THE WYE VALLEY WALK

FROM PLYNLIMON TO CHEPSTOW

by Ruth Waycott for

The Wye Valley Walk Partnership

JUNIPER HOUSE, MURLEY MOSS,
OXENHOLME ROAD, KENDAL, CUMBRIA LA9 7RL
www.cicerone.co.uk

© The Wye Valley Walk Partnership 2024

Second edition 2024
ISBN: 978 1 78631 198 6

Printed by Bell & Bain, Glasgow, on responsibly sourced paper and other controlled sources.
A catalogue record for this book is available from the British Library.
All photographs are by the author unless otherwise stated.

© Crown copyright and database rights 2024 OS AC0000810376

The Wye Valley Walk Partnership

The Wye Valley Walk is managed by a partnership of the local authorities of Powys, Herefordshire, Gloucestershire and Monmouthshire, who established and continue to maintain the route. The Wye Valley National Landscape, stretching from just south of Hereford to Chepstow, acts as the lead partner. It is the commitment and enthusiasm of staff from these organisations over 50 years that has enabled the Wye Valley Walk to be developed.

Updates to this guide

While every effort is made by our authors to ensure the accuracy of guidebooks as they go to print, changes can occur during the lifetime of an edition. Any updates that we know of for this guide will be on the Cicerone website (www.cicerone.co.uk/1198/updates), so please check before planning your trip. We also advise that you check information about such things as transport, accommodation and shops locally. Even rights of way can be altered over time. We are always grateful for information about any discrepancies between a guidebook and the facts on the ground, sent by email to updates@cicerone.co.uk or by post to Cicerone, Juniper House, Murley Moss, Oxenholme Road, Kendal LA9 7RL.

Register your book: To sign up to receive free updates, special offers and GPX files where available, create a Cicerone account and register your purchase via the 'My Account' tab at www.cicerone.co.uk.

Front cover: The approach to Ross-on-Wye (Stage 13; photo: Drew Buckley)

CONTENTS

Overview profile/staging options 6
Map key 8
Route summary table 9
Stage facilities planner 10
Preface 17

INTRODUCTION 19
The Wye Valley Walk 19
History of the Wye Valley Walk 21
The route 21

ABOUT THE WYE VALLEY 23
Landscape and history 23
The Welsh language 25
The River Wye 26
Wildlife and nature recovery 26

PLANNING YOUR TRIP 29
When to walk 29
Which way to walk? 30
Planning the walk 30
Preparing for the walk 31
Getting to and from the route 32
Transport along the route 32
Where to stay 33
What to take 34
Food and drink 34

PLANNING DAY BY DAY 36
Using this guide 36
Maps 37
Waymarking 37
The rights of way network 37
Walking with dogs 38
The Countryside Code 39
Phones and emergencies 40
Wye Valley Walk passport 40
Report a problem 41

THE WYE VALLEY WALK 42
Prologue   Reaching the start of the walk 43
Stage 1   Rhyd-y benwch to Llangurig 46
Stage 2   Llangurig to Rhayader 57
Stage 3   Rhayader to Newbridge. 66
Stage 4   Newbridge to Builth Wells 74
Stage 5   Builth Wells to Erwood 80
Stage 6   Erwood to Glasbury 90
Stage 7   Glasbury to Hay-on-Wye 97
Stage 8   Hay-on-Wye to Bredwardine. 104
Stage 9   Bredwardine to Byford 112
Stage 10   Byford to Hereford 118
Stage 11   Hereford to Fownhope 126
Stage 12   Fownhope to Ross-on-Wye 133
Stage 13   Ross-on-Wye to Kerne Bridge 144
Stage 14   Kerne Bridge to Symonds Yat. 154
Stage 15   Symonds Yat to Monmouth 163
Stage 16   Monmouth to Tintern. 169
Stage 17   Tintern to Chepstow 184

Appendix A   Tourist information and useful contacts. 194
Appendix B   Walking holiday companies and baggage transfer 196
Appendix C   Where to collect your passport stamps 197
Appendix D   Reporting a problem on a right of way 198
Appendix E   Further reading. 199
Appendix F   Selected accommodation options. 200

Keeping you on track near Hendre (Stage 1)

The Wye Valley Walk

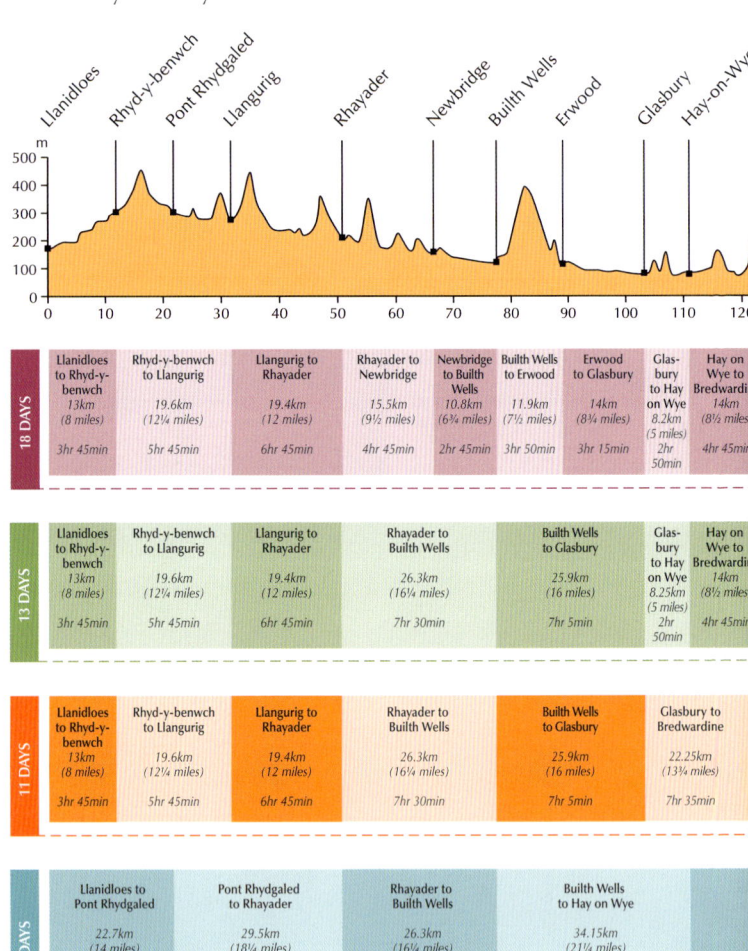

18 DAYS	Llanidloes to Rhyd-y-benwch	Rhyd-y-benwch to Llangurig	Llangurig to Rhayader	Rhayader to Newbridge	Newbridge to Builth Wells	Builth Wells to Erwood	Erwood to Glasbury	Glasbury to Hay on Wye	Hay on Wye to Bredwardine
	13km (8 miles)	*19.6km (12¼ miles)*	*19.4km (12 miles)*	*15.5km (9½ miles)*	*10.8km (6¾ miles)*	*11.9km (7½ miles)*	*14km (8¾ miles)*	*8.2km (5 miles)*	*14km (8½ miles)*
	3hr 45min	*5hr 45min*	*6hr 45min*	*4hr 45min*	*2hr 45min*	*3hr 50min*	*3hr 15min*	*2hr 50min*	*4hr 45min*

13 DAYS	Llanidloes to Rhyd-y-benwch	Rhyd-y-benwch to Llangurig	Llangurig to Rhayader	Rhayader to Builth Wells	Builth Wells to Glasbury	Glasbury to Hay on Wye	Hay on Wye to Bredwardine
	13km (8 miles)	*19.6km (12¼ miles)*	*19.4km (12 miles)*	*26.3km (16¼ miles)*	*25.9km (16 miles)*	*8.25km (5 miles)*	*14km (8½ miles)*
	3hr 45min	*5hr 45min*	*6hr 45min*	*7hr 30min*	*7hr 5min*	*2hr 50min*	*4hr 45min*

11 DAYS	Llanidloes to Rhyd-y-benwch	Rhyd-y-benwch to Llangurig	Llangurig to Rhayader	Rhayader to Builth Wells	Builth Wells to Glasbury	Glasbury to Bredwardine
	13km (8 miles)	*19.6km (12¼ miles)*	*19.4km (12 miles)*	*26.3km (16¼ miles)*	*25.9km (16 miles)*	*22.25km (13¾ miles)*
	3hr 45min	*5hr 45min*	*6hr 45min*	*7hr 30min*	*7hr 5min*	*7hr 35min*

8 DAYS	Llanidloes to Pont Rhydgaled	Pont Rhydgaled to Rhayader	Rhayader to Builth Wells	Builth Wells to Hay on Wye
	22.7km (14 miles)	*29.5km (18¼ miles)*	*26.3km (16¼ miles)*	*34.15km (21¼ miles)*
	5hr 50min	*10hr 25min*	*7hr 30min*	*9hr 55min*

OVERVIEW PROFILE/STAGING OPTIONS

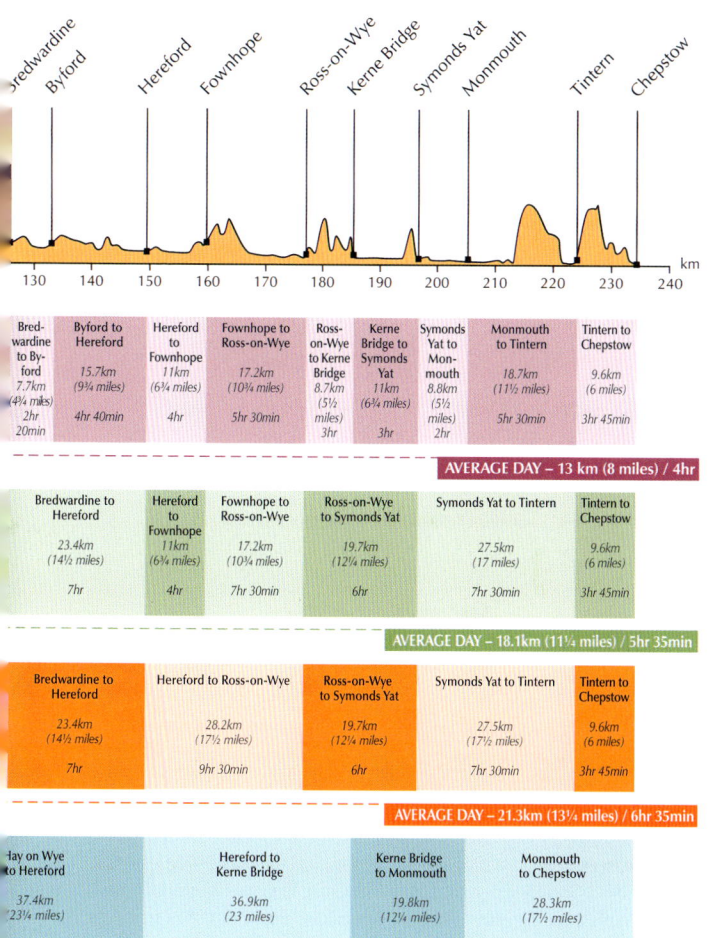

Bredwardine to Byford	Byford to Hereford	Hereford to Fownhope	Fownhope to Ross-on-Wye	Ross-on-Wye to Kerne Bridge	Kerne Bridge to Symonds Yat	Symonds Yat to Monmouth	Monmouth to Tintern	Tintern to Chepstow
7.7km (4¾ miles)	15.7km (9¾ miles)	11km (6¾ miles)	17.2km (10¾ miles)	8.7km (5½ miles)	11km (6¾ miles)	8.8km (5½ miles)	18.7km (11½ miles)	9.6km (6 miles)
2hr 20min	4hr 40min	4hr	5hr 30min	3hr	3hr	2hr	5hr 30min	3hr 45min

AVERAGE DAY – 13 km (8 miles) / 4hr

Bredwardine to Hereford	Hereford to Fownhope	Fownhope to Ross-on-Wye	Ross-on-Wye to Symonds Yat	Symonds Yat to Tintern	Tintern to Chepstow
23.4km (14½ miles)	11km (6¾ miles)	17.2km (10¾ miles)	19.7km (12¼ miles)	27.5km (17 miles)	9.6km (6 miles)
7hr	4hr	7hr 30min	6hr	7hr 30min	3hr 45min

AVERAGE DAY – 18.1km (11¼ miles) / 5hr 35min

Bredwardine to Hereford	Hereford to Ross-on-Wye	Ross-on-Wye to Symonds Yat	Symonds Yat to Tintern	Tintern to Chepstow
23.4km (14½ miles)	28.2km (17½ miles)	19.7km (12¼ miles)	27.5km (17½ miles)	9.6km (6 miles)
7hr	9hr 30min	6hr	7hr 30min	3hr 45min

AVERAGE DAY – 21.3km (13¼ miles) / 6hr 35min

Hay on Wye to Hereford	Hereford to Kerne Bridge	Kerne Bridge to Monmouth	Monmouth to Chepstow
37.4km (23¼ miles)	36.9km (23 miles)	19.8km (12¼ miles)	28.3km (17½ miles)
11hr 45min	12hr 30min	5hr	9hr 15min

AVERAGE DAY – 29.4km (18¼ miles) / 9hr

THE WYE VALLEY WALK

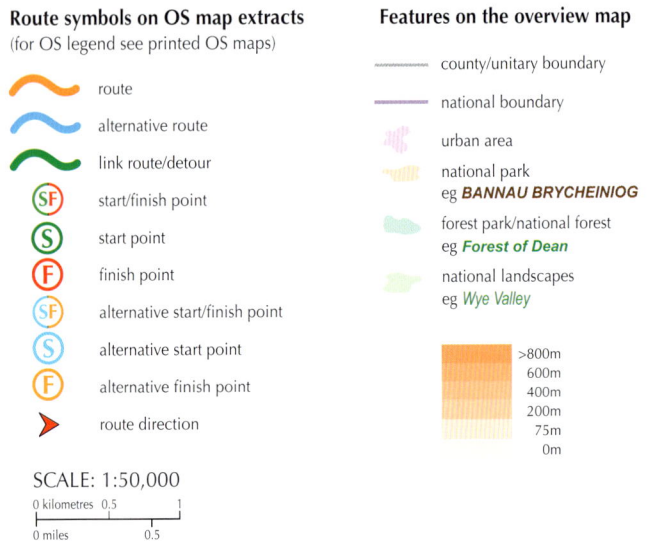

Route symbols on OS map extracts
(for OS legend see printed OS maps)

- route
- alternative route
- link route/detour
- start/finish point
- start point
- finish point
- alternative start/finish point
- alternative start point
- alternative finish point
- route direction

SCALE: 1:50,000

Features on the overview map

- county/unitary boundary
- national boundary
- urban area
- national park eg *BANNAU BRYCHEINIOG*
- forest park/national forest eg *Forest of Dean*
- national landscapes eg *Wye Valley*

>800m
600m
400m
200m
75m
0m

GPX files for all routes can be downloaded free at www.cicerone.co.uk/1198/GPX.

Acknowledgements

Thanks to all the people along the way who gave me assistance while I was researching this new source-to-sea guide to the Wye Valley Walk – from bus drivers to bag-transfer crew and the welcoming folk providing places to stay, and to everyone who stopped to chat and share their knowledge of this beautiful valley. A big 'thank you' to the volunteers who helped test the new route and to Emma for photographic expertise. Thanks also to the support crew (Paul, Briony, Lauren and Chris) who provided behind-the-scenes back up and moral support and turned up with cake on the longest day!

Thanks must also go to Powys County Council, Herefordshire Council, Gloucestershire County Council, Monmouthshire County Council, Natural Resources Wales, the Forestry Commission and the Environment Agency for their support in managing and promoting the Walk.

ROUTE SUMMARY TABLE

Stage	Start	Distance	Ascent	Time
Prologue	Llanidloes	13km (8 miles)	335m (1100ft)	3hr 45min
1	Rhyd-y-benwch	19.6km (12¼ miles)	405m (1330ft)	5hr 45min
2	Llangurig	19.4km (12 miles)	535m (1755ft)	6hr 45min
3	Rhayader	15.5km (9¾ miles)	425m (1395ft)	4hr 45min
4	Newbridge	10.8km (6¾ miles)	130m (425ft)	2hr 45min
5	Builth Wells	11.9km (7½ miles)	465m (1525ft)	3hr 50min
6	Erwood	14km (8¾ miles)	70m (230ft)	3hr 15min
7	Glasbury	8.2km (5 miles)	165m (540ft)	2hr 50min
8	Hay-on-Wye	14km (8½ miles)	440m (1445ft)	4hr 45min
9	Bredwardine	7.7km (4¾ miles)	80m (260ft)	2hr 20min
10	Byford	15.7km (9¾ miles)	135m (445ft)	4hr 40min
11	Hereford	11km (6¾ miles)	80m (260ft)	4hr
12	Fownhope	17.2km (10¾ miles)	275m (900ft)	5hr 30min
13	Ross-on-Wye	8.7km (5½ miles)	375m (1230ft)	3hr
14	Kerne Bridge	11km (6¾ miles)	250m (820ft)	3hr
15	Symonds Yat	8.8km (5½ miles)	90m (295ft)	2hr
16	Monmouth	18.7km (11½ miles)	400m (1315ft)	5hr 30min
17	Tintern	9.6km (6 miles)	470m (1540ft)	3hr 45min
Total	**Llanidloes**	**234.8km (146 miles)**	**5125m (16,815ft)**	**72hr 10min**
Total (without prologue)	**Rhyd-y-benwch**	**221.8km (137¾ miles)**	**4790m (15,715ft)**	**68hr 25min**

The Wye Valley Walk

STAGE FACILITIES PLANNER

		PROLOGUE			
Stage	Place	Walking time	Cum. stage time	Distance (km)	Cum. stage distance (km)
Start	Llanidloes	0hr	0hr	0km	0km
Finish	Rhyd-y-benwch	3hr 45min	3hr 45min	13km	13km

		WYE VALLEY WALK			
Stage	Place	Walking time	Cum. stage time	Distance (km)	Cum. stage distance (km)
Start	Rhyd-y-benwch	0hr	0hr	0km	0km
1	*Penlon (Hendre)*			12.8km (+0.8km)	12.8km (+0.8km)
1	Plas Bwlch (Ty-mawr)			1.2km (+1km)	14km (+1km)
1	*Glangwy*			2.3km (+0.1km)	16.3km (+0.1km)
1	**Llangurig**	**5hr 45min**	**5hr 45min**	**3.3km**	**19.6km**
2	Clochfaen	15min	15min	1km	1km
2	Coed Cochion	6hr	6hr 15min	16km	17km
2	**Rhayader**	**30min**	**6hr 45min**	**2.4km**	**19.4km**
3	*Doliago Farm (Dolgai)*			6km (+0.6km)	6km (+0.6km)
3	*Doldowlod (Llanwrthwl)*			0.7km (+1km)	6.7km (+1km)
3	**Newbridge**	**4hr 45min**	**4hr 45min**	**8.8km**	**15.5km**
4	*Cilmeri*			6.4km (+4km)	6.4km (+4km)
4	**Builth Wells**	**2hr 45min**	**2hr 45min**	**4.4km**	**10.8km**
5	Pantypyllau			4km	4km
5	Erwood Village			6.6km (+0.2km)	10.6km (+0.2km)
5	*Pwll-y-faedda B&B*			1km (+0.4km)	11.6km (+0.4km)

Stage Facilities Planner

- ⭕ Hotel/B&B/guesthouse
- ⬆ Hostel/bunkhouse
- 🔺 Campsite
- 🍴 Refreshments (meals available)
- 🛒 Grocery shop
- 👕 Outdoor shop
- ⬛ Train
- 🔵 Bus
- 🔳 ATM

Facilities								
Hotel	Hostel	Campsite	Refreshments	Grocery	Outdoor	Train	Bus	ATM
⭕	⬆	🔺	🍴	🛒			🔵	🔳

Facilities								
Hotel	Hostel	Campsite	Refreshments	Grocery	Outdoor	Train	Bus	ATM
⭕								
⭕								
		🔺						
⭕			🍴	🛒			🔵	
⭕								
		🔺						
⭕		🔺	🍴	🛒			🔵	🔳
		🔺						
			🍴	🛒			🔵	
⭕		🔺	🍴	🛒			🔵	
⭕			🍴			⬛	🔵	
⭕		🔺	🍴	🛒	👕	⬛	🔵	🔳
⭕								
⭕			🍴				🔵	
⭕								

THE WYE VALLEY WALK

Stage	Place	Walking time	Cum. stage time	Distance (km)	Cum. stage distance (km)
5	The Skreen			0.2km (+0.3km)	11.8km (+0.3km)
5	Great House Farm, Llandeilo Graben			0km	11.8km (+1.8km)
5	**Erwood Station Craft Centre**	**3hr 50min**	**3hr 50min**	**0.1km**	**11.9km**
6	Llangoed Hall Hotel			5.8km (+0.3km)	5.8km (+0.3km)
6	Boughrood	2hr 5min	2hr 5min	2.2km	8km
6	Lyswen			0km (+0.6km)	8km (+0.6km)
6	**Glasbury**	**1hr 10min**	**3hr 15min**	**6km**	**14km**
7	Llowes	1hr	1hr	3.2km	3.2km
7	**Hay-on-Wye**	**1hr 50min**	**2hr 50min**	**5km**	**8.2km**
8	Drover's Road (Llanerch-y-coed)			4.2km (+4km)	4.2km (+4km)
8	Locksters Pool			2.2km (+0.4km)	6.4km (+0.4km)
8	Whitney on Wye			0km (+3.3km)	6.4km (+3.3km)
8	Pen-y-park			1.3km (+4km)	7.7km (4km)
8	**Bredwardine**	**4hr 45min**	**4hr 45min**	**6.3km**	**14km**
9	Brobury House Gardens	15min	15min	1km	1km
8	Dairy House Farm B&B			2.4km (+0.4km)	3.4km (+0.4km)
8	Byford Glamping			4.2km (+0.5km)	7.6km (0.5km)
9	**Byford**	**2hr 5min**	**2hr 20min**	**0.1km**	**7.7km**
10	Credenhill			4.7km (+1km)	4.7km (+1km)
10	The Priory			0km (+3km)	4.7km (+3km)
10	**Hereford**	**4hr 40min**	**4hr 40min**	**11km**	**15.7km**
11	Mordiford			8km (+0.1km)	8km (+0.1km)

Stage facilities planner

		Facilities					
⭕							
⭕	🟢						
⭕		🍴				⬤ (Hail at Erwood Bridge)	
⭕		🍴					
		🍴	🛒			⬤	
⭕		🍴	🛒			⬤	
⭕	🟢	🍴	🛒			⬤	
	🟢					⬤	
⭕	🟢	🍴	🛒	🏪		⬤	🅿
⭕	🟢						
	🟢						
⭕	🟢						
⭕							
⭕		🍴					
		🍴					
⭕							
⭕	🟢						
		🍴	🛒				
⭕							
⭕	🟢	🍴	🛒	🏪	⬤	⬤	🅿
	🟢						

THE WYE VALLEY WALK

Stage	Place	Walking time	Cum. stage time	Distance (km)	Cum. stage distance (km)
11	**Fownhope**	**4hr**	**4hr**	**3km**	**11km**
12	Caplor Farm	1hr 10min	1hr 10min	3.6km	3.6km
12	How Caple	1hr 30min	2hr 40min	4.8km	8.4km
12	*Townsend Farm*			*5.8km (1km)*	*14.2km (+1km)*
12	**Ross-on-Wye**	**2hr 50min**	**5hr 30min**	**3km**	**17.2km**
13	**Kerne Bridge**	**3hr**	**3hr**	**8.7km**	**8.7km**
14	Welsh Bicknor	1hr 20min	1hr 20min	5.5km	5.5km
14	Symonds Yat Rock	1hr 30min	2hr 50min	4.5km	10km
14	**Symonds Yat**	**10min**	**3hr**	**1km**	**11km**
15	Biblins	30min	30min	2km	2km
15	**Monmouth**	**1hr 30min**	**2hr**	**6.8km**	**8.8km**
16	Redbrook	1hr 10min	1hr 10min	4.5km	4.5km
16	*Whitebrook*			*3.75km (+1km)*	*8.25km (+1km)*
16	*New Mills*			*0km (+3km)*	*8.25km (+3km)*
16	*Brockweir*			*7.75km (+1km)*	*16km (+1km)*
16	**Tintern**	**3hr 20min**	**5hr 30min**	**2.7km**	**18.7km**
Finish	Chepstow	3hr 45min	3hr 45min	9.6km	9.6km

STAGE FACILITIES PLANNER

		Facilities					
🛏️		🍴	🛁			⬛	
	🏕️					⬛	
	🏕️						
	🏕️	🍴	🛁				
🛏️	🏕️	🍴	🛁	👕		⬛	🔲
🛏️		🍴				⬛	
⬆		🍴					
		🍴					
🛏️	🏕️	🍴					
	🏕️						
🛏️	🏕️	🍴	🛁	👕		⬛	🔲
🛏️		🍴	🛁			⬛	
🛏️		🍴					
🛏️	🏕️						
		🍴				⬛	
🛏️		🍴	🛁			⬛	
🛏️		🍴	🛁		🟥	⬛	🔲

15

Taking in the Black Mountains (Stage 5; photo: Emma Drabble)

PREFACE BY KATE HUMBLE

The Wye Valley Walk passes through this beautiful part of the world which I am lucky enough to call home. Don't rush the walk. The route often climbs away from the river providing a different perspective on the unfolding landscapes that are frequently, and sometimes literally, breathtaking. Remember to stop once in a while and take in your magnificent surroundings.

Kate Humble

Kate and Teg enjoying the Wye Valley Walk (photo: Drew Buckley)

Approaching Llowes (Stage 7; photo Emma Drabble)

INTRODUCTION

Tranquil waters passing Perrystone (Stage 12; photo: Gemma Kate Wood)

THE WYE VALLEY WALK

The Wye Valley Walk is one of the most admired river trails in the UK, with walkers travelling from around the world to enjoy this classic long-distance source-to-sea route. It offers a perfect mix of riverside and hill walking, following the valley of the Wye for 222km as the river descends some 680m from its source high in the mountains of Mid Wales, to where it flows into the Severn just below Chepstow. It's a journey of contrasts, from the crystal clear stream on the remote and rugged uplands of Plynlimon, to the tidal, muddy estuary flowing past dramatic limestone cliffs at Chepstow, which has the third highest tides in the world.

The Walk actually begins beside the River Severn, one of three sister rivers having their source on Plynlimon. Legend has it the sisters chose different routes to the sea: the Rheidol picked the fastest route to Cardigan Bay, the Severn took the longest route, while the Wye chose the prettiest route, which you will soon be able to confirm as true! It's also a walk that weaves across the border between Wales and England five times, although you won't need your passport for these crossings. The path doesn't stick faithfully to the river, for no matter how gorgeous the river may be, walking beside it reveals only one side of its character. You have to climb up the valley sides, gain

Rapids on the Upper Wye (photo: Adam Fisher)

height and distance, to really appreciate a river in its landscape.

Plynlimon, or Pumlumon in Welsh, is the highest point of the Cambrian Mountains, and offers unsurpassed hillwalking and extensive views. The Walk heads south through landscapes of upland moorland and quiet valleys, dotted with farms, where the historic Welsh market towns of Rhayader and Builth Wells provide welcoming overnight stops. The Black Mountains and Bannau Brycheiniog (Brecon Beacons) are spotted for the first time near Erwood. At Hay-on-Wye, the world famous 'town of books', the Walk leaves behind the brooding mountains and crosses the border into England, passing through the gentler, red-earthed farming countryside of the Herefordshire Plain with its rolling hills, cider orchards and historic Hereford cattle. The city of Hereford is the largest settlement on the Wye Valley Walk and is home to a magnificent 11th-century cathedral.

South of Hereford the last 85km of the Walk pass through the Wye Valley National Landscape, an area of outstanding natural beauty providing a spectacular finale of dramatic limestone gorges, dazzling viewpoints and romantic ruins. At Ross-on-Wye follow in the footsteps of earlier Wye tourists at the starting point for the famed Wye Tour. The striking limestone gorge scenery at Symonds Yat Rock is one of the most iconic panoramas on the Walk. Crossing the border back into Wales the river flows into its final stunning gorge section south of Monmouth, where ancient woodland, which turns orange and gold in autumn, clads the hillsides. On the final stage the remarkable ruins of Tintern Abbey are passed, immortalised by William Wordsworth in his *Lines Composed a Few Miles Above Tintern Abbey*. The path climbs high above the river to reach views from the Eagle's Nest and the Giant's Cave on the Piercefield estate. Say a final farewell to your companion for the last 222km as the Wye flows beneath Chepstow's clifftop castle and out into the Severn under the old Severn Bridge.

HISTORY OF THE WYE VALLEY WALK

Work started on creating the path in 1975 with the first sections established between Chepstow, Monmouth and Ross-on-Wye. Over the years the route progressed through Herefordshire and into Powys. The final section to Plynlimon and Hafren Forest, close to the source of the Wye, was completed in 2003. The Wye Valley Walk Partnership is a collaboration between the four local authorities the Walk passes through (Powys, Herefordshire, Gloucestershire and Monmouthshire) who maintain the route, and the Wye Valley National Landscape Team, covering the area south of Hereford to Chepstow.

THE ROUTE

Upper reaches of the Wye

The Wye Valley Walk soon leaves Hafren Forest to cross the open slopes of Plynlimon, where there is a real sense of remoteness and isolation – wide exposed skies, boggy moorland and dramatic far-reaching views to the peaks of Eryri (Snowdonia) in the north and the Cambrian Mountains to the west. During the breeding season skylarks sing high above the flocks of hardy Welsh mountain sheep that graze the open mountain tops during summer but are moved down to fields closer to farmhouses in winter. Buzzard, peregrine falcon and red kite are usually easy to spot. If you are lucky you might even see migrating ospreys that nest in Hafren Forest. It is a couple of hours walk from the start of the Walk at Rhyd-y-benwch before you catch your first sight of the Wye, a tiny shallow stream falling over sections of rocky cascades that becomes a small river by the time it reaches Llangurig.

Although it might feel like this is the highest point on the Wye Valley Walk, you won't reach that until Stage 2 when you cross Nantyhendy Hill at 480m, where traditional Welsh Black cattle graze in summer. This is another remote upland landscape with 360-degree views. Stage 2 is full of delights: the peaceful Dernol Valley; unusual stone slab fences at Safn-y-coed; the traditional Welsh longhouse at Gilfach Nature Reserve; heather-clad hills; and the beautiful River Marteg. The final area of open upland to be crossed in the upper reaches of the Wye is on Stage 5 at Banc y Celyn between Builth Wells and Erwood, where the views towards the Black Mountains in the far distance really do make your heart sing.

The middle Wye

South of Erwood the river valley widens and the views open up with a fleeting glimpse of the Bannau

Brycheiniog. There is now an expansive flood plain and the river is much wider, sometimes flowing slow and deep, other times tumbling over rapids. Confronted by the Black Mountains below Boughrood, the Wye changes direction, flowing northeast to Hay-on-Wye, where it enters England for the first (but not last) time and the path, like the Wye, meanders across the Herefordshire Plain. There's one last big climb to the top of Merbach Hill at just over 318m. Distinctive rich red and white Hereford cattle replace the sheep of the earlier upland hill farms as the path rambles through rolling arable fields and orchards.

Perfect soil and weather combine in Herefordshire to grow the finest apples and pears, making the county the largest producer of cider in the country. One moment you are walking through apple orchards and fields and the next you have arrived, along the riverbank, in the only city on the Wye. Hereford is a relaxed place packed with history. A stone's throw from the river, the cathedral is home to the largest surviving medieval map of the world, the 800-year-old Mappa Mundi, and the largest remaining chained library. Alongside the Black and White House Museum, the Museum of Cider and the Waterworks Museum, there is more than enough to fill a rest (or rainy) day.

The lower Wye and the Wye Valley National Landscape

South of Hereford the final 85km of the Wye Valley Walk passes through the Wye Valley National Landscape, designated in 1971 to protect the special qualities of this area of outstanding natural beauty which straddles the Wales-England border. National Landscapes have the same level of protection as National Parks and work to conserve and enhance the natural beauty of the area. The Wye Valley National Landscape has become one of the best-known and most-visited landscapes in southern Britain.

The oldest rocks in the region are the Silurian limestones and sandstones that make up the grey soils of the Woolhope Dome in the north of the National Landscape. Old Red Sandstone from the younger Devonian period creates the fertile red and brown soils of the Herefordshire lowlands, along with the rich alluvium of the floodplain. These softer rocks allowed the river to meander more widely. From Lydbrook the river cuts in and out of the harder Carboniferous Limestone to form dramatic gorges with sheer cliffs and steeply wooded slopes at Symonds Yat. Between Monmouth and Chepstow the woods are at their most impressive, creating a stunning backdrop to the river as it flows past Tintern Abbey and Chepstow's medieval castle. It's a landscape particularly rich in history.

ABOUT THE WYE VALLEY

The Welsh flag

LANDSCAPE AND HISTORY

Hillforts above the Wye

This border region has been fought over for thousands of years, its strategic importance reflected in a strong defensive landscape dating back to the Iron Age. On the Wye Valley Walk between Hereford and Chepstow you will pass nine Iron Age hillforts constructed between 700BC and 43AD. The Silures were the dominant Celtic tribe in south east Wales until they were subdued by the Romans around AD74. We don't know if the Wye actually marked the border between the Silures and their neighbours the Dobunni, or whether these hillforts were designed to control the River Wye itself and its valuable trade. But there are pairs of hillforts – Piercefield facing Spital Meend and Symonds Yat facing the Little Doward – as well as a promontory fort at Bulwark, which controlled the mouth of the Wye.

Welsh or English?

After the Romans left, the Welsh kingdom of Ergyng stretched across what is now southern Herefordshire and parts of Monmouthshire and Gloucestershire, from the Black Mountains to the Forest of Dean and down the lower Wye Valley. Hereford, which today is some 32km from the Welsh border, was well and truly located inside the Welsh kingdom. Ergyng became a stronghold of the old Celtic church and one of its last outposts in Britain because it was so remote from the invading pagan Saxons. Hints of early Celtic church sites can be found in local place names beginning with 'Llan' – the old Welsh word for a church or cemetery.

The massive defensive structure of Offa's Dyke stretching from 'sea to sea' (Severn to Dee), was built by King Offa in the 8th century to mark the boundary between his kingdom of Mercia and the Welsh kingdoms. It influenced where the national boundary is today. In the lower Wye Valley the Dyke runs between Lydbrook and Chepstow, high above the Wye on the English side of the river.

Following the Norman invasion of 1066, defences against the Welsh kingdoms were bolstered by the English Norman kings, who gave land along the border to Norman lords to act as a buffer zone. More than 400 castles were built to control the Marches, with Norman fortresses along the Wye from Builth Wells down to Chepstow. 'Marcher' is an old Norman word referring to the border between Normandy and Brittany, brought over by the Normans, who used it to describe the Welsh border country. These castles are a highly visible symbol of the power battles played out between Norman lords and the Welsh kingdoms until the Welsh were finally defeated in 1283.

Industrial heritage

The lower Wye Valley and Forest of Dean have an iron industry pre-dating the Romans. It was one of the earliest places in the UK to industrialise and by 1600 the wireworks at Tintern were the largest industrial enterprise in Wales, employing hundreds of people. Fast-flowing streams cascading off the surrounding plateau were harnessed to power waterwheels. Iron, copper and tin works belching smoke into the valley consumed vast quantities of charcoal produced from local timber. The Wye made it easy to import raw materials and export manufactured goods. It was a watery highway linking the riverside villages with the wider world, as boatmen navigated trows laden with cargo. Quays dotted the villages along the Wye between Hay and Chepstow, where the associated trades of shipbuilding and boat repairs, rope and sail making developed. River trade declined with the coming of the railway in the 1870s. The closure of the railway in the mid-20th century led to the decline of the valley's industry too. The last metal works in the Wye Valley, a tinplate factory at Redbrook, shut in 1968.

Much of this industrial heritage has been lost, but at Abbey Furnace in Tintern's Angidy Valley you can view the excavated and partly restored remains of the 17th-century ironworks. Built in 1672–73 to produce the special osmond iron needed to make wire, it was a vital component in the Tintern wireworks complex. The 8km Angidy Trail explores Tintern's hidden industry, taking in the furnace, forge and wireworks, workers' cottages, limekilns, tidal dock and the church where generations of metal workers were baptised, married and buried. Download information at www.wyevalley-nl.org.uk.

In search of the picturesque

The lower Wye Valley has long been recognised as an area of exceptional landscape quality. Cistercian monks appreciated both the productive potential and the tranquillity of this landscape when they founded Tintern Abbey on the banks of the Wye. In the 18th century the Wye Valley was the first of Britain's great landscapes to be 'discovered' and it was here that British tourism was born with the development of the Wye Tour. This two-day boat trip down the river to Chepstow was the height of fashion in the late 18th and early 19th centuries when painters, poets and writers came in search of the picturesque. The popularity of the Tour was a direct result of the first illustrated travel guide to be published in Britain in 1782, *Observations on the River Wye* by William Gilpin. He was a pioneer in the appreciation of landscape in Britain, developing a set of rules for 'picturesque' beauty. Landscape appreciation and conservation have grown out of Gilpin's ideas and his influence contributed to the creation of the National Trust in 1906 and the designation of National Parks and National Landscapes after 1949.

THE WELSH LANGUAGE

Welsh is one of Europe's oldest living languages and Wales is a bilingual nation where Welsh enjoys official language status alongside English and is spoken by around 18 per cent of the population. You will be more likely to hear Welsh spoken in Mid Wales than along the more anglicised border, but

Redbrook was Britain's copper capital in the 18th century (Stage 16)

Welsh is all around you on the Walk, especially in place names. Even on the English side of the border you could be forgiven for thinking you are in Wales as every other village has a Welsh name or anglicised version of it, reflecting the historical changes in the boundary.

THE RIVER WYE

The Wye is designated as a Special Area of Conservation (SAC) as well as being the first major river to be designated along its entire length as a Site of Special Scientific Interest (SSSI). In 2010 it was voted the nation's favourite river and was regularly described as one of the most natural rivers in the UK. By 2023, however, local communities, celebrities and TV programmes were protesting about pollution, which was having a catastrophic impact on the Wye and its wildlife. Salmon catches in the river have declined by 94 per cent and the species is now on the International Union for Conservation of Nature (IUCN) Red List of Threatened Species. Climate change and land use changes in Powys and Herefordshire, including farm intensification and the proliferation of poultry sheds, sewage discharges, higher temperatures and increased flooding events has seen water crowfoot, an important indicator species for the health of the river, decline by 90 per cent. The concentration of phosphates has also led to damaging algae blooms.

Water quality has become an extremely contentious issue. In May 2023, the River Wye Site of Special Scientific Interest and River Wye Special Area of Conservation was downgraded from 'unfavourable recovering' to 'unfavourable declining' by Natural England, due to the decline in key species including Atlantic salmon, aquatic plants such as water crowfoot and native white-clawed crayfish. These issues affect most of the tributaries of the Wye from the River Marteg (just above Rhayader) downstream. The Wye is not the only river suffering from pollution, but action to raise awareness of the state of the UK's rivers does seem to have been focused on the Wye. There is hope. Local campaigners have done much to put the river's plight in the public domain. All the stakeholders are recognising the problem. Concerted collaborative actions to restore the Wye catchment to a healthy condition have begun, but it will take many years to mitigate and reverse the damage.

WILDLIFE AND NATURE RECOVERY

Plynlimon is one of the most important upland areas for nature conservation in Wales, especially for its moorland habitat and high mountain plants. Led by Montgomery Wildlife Trust, the Pumlumon Project stretches across 40,000ha of Cambrian Mountains' heathland, blanket bog,

WILDLIFE AND NATURE RECOVERY

woodland, conifer plantation and grassland. Since 2007 the project has been pioneering an upland economy built around wildlife, ecology and long-term sustainability.

Gilfach Nature Reserve is an old hill farm with the River Marteg running through it. The diversity of wildlife here is amazing, including 413 types of lichen, more than 25 per cent of the total number of lichens found in Wales. Small numbers of Welsh Whites, Galloway cattle and Welsh mountain sheep graze the reserve to help create different habitats. 70 different birds have been recorded including redpoll, yellow hammer, whinchat, linnet, red kite, spotted flycatcher and cuckoo, with pied flycatchers, dippers and redstarts found along the river.

Limestone cliffs towering above the river are a distinctive feature of the Wye Valley National Landscape. These inaccessible cliffs provide feeding, nesting and breeding areas for spectacular birds of prey, including goshawks, buzzards and peregrine falcons. Peregrines were on the verge of extinction in the 1960s due to human persecution and pesticides. The first pair to nest here in the 1970s became the focal point of a successful Royal Society for the Protection of Birds conservation programme and since then greater legal protection, and the banning of DDT, has helped numbers recover. Peregrines can be seen at Yat Rock from early spring throughout the breeding season. Goshawks have

Reintroduced pine martens have successfully bred (photo: Alasdair Sargent)

also faced much persecution, but the Welsh borders and Forest of Dean are one of few places where they are still doing well. Rare whitebeams and sessile oaks grow on the limestone cliffs, while an area of limestone pavement on the Little Doward provides important habitats for lime-loving plants and animals.

The Lower Wye Valley woodlands are one of largest and most important areas of native woodland remaining in Britain. Below Monmouth almost 40 per cent of the Wye Valley National Landscape is woodland (compared to only 13 per cent across the UK) with woods lining the banks of the Wye for nearly 28km. Over 1000 hectares of ancient semi-natural broadleaved woodland has been designated as a

Special Area of Conservation, protecting very rare insect species including Cosnard's net-winged beetle, only found at Piercefield in Wales. These woodlands also support significant populations of bats. Thirteen of the 17 UK bat species and 27 per cent of the UK population of lesser horseshoe bats live in this area with nine roosting sites for greater and lesser horseshoe bats designated as a Special Area of Conservation. The tiny and fast-flying lesser horseshoe, weighing the same as a 10p coin, is one of the rarest UK bat species.

The Wye Valley National Landscape is also important for species-rich grassland. Floodplain meadows, especially in spring and summer when full of grasses and wildflowers, provide vital habitat for insects and birds. They are now very rare as a result of intensive farming, but the Wye Valley National Landscape is working with local farmers to restore and create flower-rich grasslands along the Wye. Floodplain grasslands have other benefits, storing carbon deep in the soils, regulating water flows and flooding. Along the 15-mile tidal section of the river are stretches of marshy grassland and mudflats with estuarine habitats supporting species such as sea aster, seaside centaury and water dropwort.

Reintroductions are playing a bigger role in nature recovery with pine martens and beavers having been successfully reintroduced in the lower Wye Valley in 2018, along with the unofficial release of boar in the Forest of Dean. The focus is on connectivity, not just restoring and expanding priority sites, but connecting landscapes so that species can spread between areas. The Wye has huge potential to connect wildlife and nature in this way.

Invasive species

As well as pollution, invasive non-native species are an issue along the Wye. If you walk during the summer months, you will inevitably pass the sweet-smelling pink flowers of Himalayan balsam. It is the most dominant invasive plant in the Wye Valley, taking over long stretches of the Wye and its tributaries. It outcompetes native riverside wildflowers such as common comfrey, purple loosestrife, great willowherb and meadowsweet and when the balsam dies back in winter it leaves the riverbanks bare and vulnerable to erosion. Each plant can produce 2500 seeds, which are easily transported downstream by the river, multiplying the problem. Japanese knotweed, giant hogweed and American skunk cabbage are also problematic where they occur. The Wye Valley National Landscape Team supports projects to tackle these issues, but as only 8 per cent of the Wye's catchment is within the National Landscape, the problem is coordinating activities in the other 92 per cent of the catchment.

PLANNING YOUR TRIP

Spring in the Wye Valley (photo: Gemma Kate Wood)

WHEN TO WALK

You can walk at any time of year, but some sections of the route may be flooded, muddy or slippery after heavy rain and the upland moorland sections may be snow-covered in winter. Later in summer, paths may become overgrown with vegetation, while bracken often takes over upland paths. Farm crops may also interfere with easy access on some field paths. Do report any issues you find along the way to ensure the route is kept open.

Spring
In the south the Wye Valley bursts into bloom in April and May. Bluebells put on an unforgettable floor show of stunning blues along with a heady perfume. In the tree canopy above, lime green leaves unfurl in the spring sunshine. Woodland paths are lined with wild garlic and wood anemone. Spring may arrive a little later in the upland areas further north, while Herefordshire's cider orchards start blossoming from late March for six weeks or so.

Summer
Summer brings traditional wildflower meadows swaying in the breeze, the smell of hay making, skylarks singing and, if you are lucky, the peculiar sound of nightjars calling as darkness falls. Striking stands of purple foxgloves and bay willow herb accompany you along the walk and, in late summer, a blaze of yellow gorse and

a purple haze of heather clads the upland hilltops.

Autumn

Autumn brings the best displays of 'dragon's breath', as humid air and cool, clear nights are required for this phenomenon to form. When the water in the Wye is warmer than the surrounding air, wispy streaks of mist hover above the river. Sometimes the river looks like it is steaming, other times denser drifts of fog cover the whole valley, shifting as the sun warms the day up. (Dragon's breath can occur at any time of the year when the conditions are right.) Add in the fabulous autumnal reds, golds and oranges of the ancient woodlands and an autumnal walk in the Wye can be spectacular. However, it can (and does) rain, paths may be muddy and slippery and walking days shorter as the nights draw in.

Winter

Crisp frosty mornings and crystal clear views can be the rewards of winter walking in the Wye Valley. As the trees have lost their leaves the views are better, while early winter sunsets provide a stunning end to a (shorter) day's walking. The Wye does flood at times after extended periods of rain, usually late autumn, winter and early spring. High water alternate routes are detailed in the relevant sections. Check river levels and flood alerts at https://riverlevels.uk.

WHICH WAY TO WALK?

This guide is written from source to sea (north to south) and most people choose to walk in this direction as it feels 'right' to finish at the sea (sort of). There are more practical benefits to finishing the walk in Chepstow – you can celebrate your achievement in a local pub or restaurant and catch a train home from the railway station (rather than being stranded in the middle of nowhere without mobile phone signal). However, you can walk in either direction. The path is waymarked and clearly marked on OS maps, so if you prefer to start at the sea and walk to the source you can. There is no right or wrong way! You need to factor in reaching the start of the walk at Rhyd-y-benwch (or leaving the end of the walk if walking south to north), which is 13km from the nearest town at Llanidloes. See 'Getting to and from the route' and the Prologue stage.

PLANNING THE WALK

There are many ways to walk the Wye. The 'all in one go' walkers stride straight through from Rhyd-y-Benwch to Chepstow in as little as seven days, but 10 or 12 days are more usual, and a halfway rest day is always recommended. You may like the independence of camping and carrying your own tent, although campsites are not always conveniently located at the end of a section (and wild camping is not allowed in England and Wales). Alternatively, holidays featuring the

PREPARING FOR THE WALK

Wye Valley Walk are offered by several walking holiday operators who will be happy to sort out all the logistics. See Appendix B and www.wyevalleywalk.org for details.

Others find it logistically better to split the walk into several trips which start and end within striking distance of a railway station, for example Rhyd-y-benwch (nearest station Caersws) to Builth Wells (nearest station Builth Road), Builth Wells to Hereford and Hereford to Chepstow (both have stations). Taking a long weekend to cover two or three stages, staying in local accommodation and having your bags transferred to the next hotel each morning may offer more appeal. People living close to the route often choose to walk single sections at a time, ticking off the miles to suit.

You might even want to mix it up and add in a canoe or stand-up paddle boarding adventure on one or two of the stages along the navigable river, for instance between Hereford and Hoarwithy or Kerne Bridge and Monmouth.

PREPARING FOR THE WALK

The Wye Valley Walk is not difficult or challenging for most of its length but there are some steep rocky sections, potentially muddy hillsides, paths with riverside drops and exposed mountain uplands. Make sure you are prepared and properly equipped. Know your own fitness level and plan a walk that suits you. If you are walking alone let someone know where you're going and where and when

Bluebells and ransoms (wild garlic) add to the joy of walking in spring (Stage 2; photo: Gemma Kate Wood)

you expect to arrive at your destination. Learn to read a map, so you can find your way when fog or low cloud obscures visibility, or you need to give the grid reference of your location in an emergency. What3words is a useful app to download in case of emergency too, as it can assist in finding your location: https://what3words.com.

waymarked route from Llanidloes to Rhyd-y-benwch. If you are walking from sea to source and this is your final stage note that there is no mobile phone signal at Rhyd-y-benwch to call a taxi when you finish, so be sure to make arrangements before setting out. Llanidloes is well served by buses that connect with the nearest railway stations at Caersws and Newtown.

GETTING TO AND FROM THE ROUTE

There is no public transport to reach the start of the Walk at remote Rhyd-y-benwch and Llanidloes, the nearest town, is 13km away. To avoid adding extra mileage to the first day's walking many people arrange a drop-off at the start by friends, family or a local Llanidloes taxi company. Alternatively, you can arrive on foot by taking the Severn Way, a 13km

TRANSPORT ALONG THE ROUTE

Buses serve most of the towns and villages en route (including Llanidloes, Llangurig, Rhayader, Builth Wells, Erwood, Glasbury, Hay-on-Wye, Bredwardine, Hereford, Mordiford, Fownhope, Ross-on-Wye, Kerne Bridge, Monmouth, Redbrook, Tintern and Chepstow) but these services may be minimal. Many rural

Misty view below Symonds Yat Rock (Stage 14; photo Ed Moskalenko)

services operate a hail and ride system, meaning passengers may be picked up or set down at any point on the route provided it is safe to do so. Look out for the bus and as it approaches raise your arm to signal to the driver you wish to board. Buses may not stop at every bus stop, so tell the driver you wish to alight, either by using the bell or asking in advance.

There are train stations at Caersws (closest to the start) on the Cambrian Line between Shrewsbury and Aberystwyth, Builth Road (5km off the path north of Builth Wells), or Cilmeri (4km off the path to the west of Builth Wells), on the Heart of Wales Line between Shrewsbury and Swansea, Hereford on the Welsh Marches Line between Shrewsbury and Newport and Chepstow on the Gloucester to Newport line.

The closest airports to the start are Liverpool, Birmingham and Manchester and nearest to the finish are Bristol and Cardiff.

WHERE TO STAY

Book accommodation in advance, unless you have nerves of steel! With limited public transport you don't want to have to travel far at the end of a day's walking, especially in the evening or on a Sunday when most buses do not run. If you ask, some B&B owners will pick you up from the route and drop you back the following morning. Ad hoc and planned events can fill local accommodation quickly, with Hay Festival (end of May/early June) and the Royal Welsh Show (July) filling much of the accommodation within a 40km radius of these towns. You could book self-catering

accommodation for a few days to tackle three or four stages, if you can sort out getting to the start and from the finish each day by bus, taxi or using two cars. Or ask if you can stay for one night for a small supplement, which may be acceptable during the off-season.

You will find all sorts of places to stay, from shepherd's huts nestled under the trees in apple orchards, to back-to-nature campsites where the skies are dark and stars twinkle free from light pollution. There's even a riverside city-centre campsite just minutes off the Wye Valley Walk. There are two YHA hostels, one housed in a grand old rectory looking out over the river at Welsh Bicknor and another in a medieval castle at St Briavels. At the other end of the scale, you could push the boat out at a Michelin starred restaurant with rooms, only five minutes off the path in Whitebrook. In between you will find comfy B&Bs and hotels used to walkers arriving wet, cold and sometimes muddy. Find details of places to stay at: www.wyevalleywalk.org/plan/stay.

WHAT TO TAKE

Lightweight walking boots and waterproof clothing are essential. Even in summer waterproof trousers are a boon when walking through long grass on a wet day. Your backpack should contain extra layers of warm clothing, sun protection, mobile phone, OS maps, compass, GPS, camera, first aid kit, your Cicerone Guide and enough food and drink for the day's walking. Check the weather forecast before you begin your walk each day, so that you are adequately dressed and prepared: www.metoffice.gov.uk. Some parts of the route can be exposed to high winds, with little shelter from wind, rain and sun, and feel unpleasant even in summer without warm and waterproof clothing.

To save carrying all your gear, baggage transfers can be arranged along the route. See Appendix B and www.wyevalleywalk.org for details of companies offering this service.

Travellers taking the Wye Tour in the late 18th century had a very specific luggage list for their expedition: a copy of William Gilpin's guidebook to the Wye, pedometer, telescope, barometer, maps, tour journals, sketch books, watercolours, a pocket edition of William Cowper's poems and a Claude glass. You probably don't need such a lengthy list today!

FOOD AND DRINK

Most sections on the Walk start and finish in a small town or village where you can find food and drink supplies, if somewhat limited. However, if you arrive late in the day the local village shop will probably be closed and pubs and restaurants may stop serving food early, so check serving times in advance. Stages where there are no food and drink stops are identified in each stage information section so you can plan ahead and, if need be, request

Food and drink

a packed lunch from your accommodation. There is a bit of a 'black hole' between Hay-on-Wye and Hereford so plan ahead for these sections. Take enough water for the day, with extra on hot days, and don't be tempted to fill up water bottles from streams.

A good day's walk can be made even better with a welcome food stop – there's nothing nicer than trying local food and drink so a few suggestions are made here of places on, or very close to, the route. Great Oak Foods in Llanidloes is a good place to stock up at the start of the Walk. It is a community shop selling fresh, organic and locally grown produce, cheeses, wines, beers, cider, artisan bread and cakes. Shepherds Parlour coffee shop and ice cream parlour in Hay-on-Wye is definitely not to be missed. While in Hereford, meat lovers should look out for The Beefy Boys, set up by four backyard amateur cooks with a passion for local produce, while cheese lovers will be well-catered for in the Mousetrap, a specialist cheese shop on pretty Church Street.

You can't get more local than Herefordshire cider. Ross-on-Wye Cider & Perry Company grow 100 varieties of apples and 30 varieties of pears on their orchards at Peterstow and make more than 50 ciders and perries. Near Walford, the Walk passes through the vines at Wythall Estate Vineyard, which grow in a unique micro-climate created by the undulating terrain (experienced on the Walk as steep down and even steeper up). They open for tours and tastings during summer months and their wines are on the menu at the nearby Hostelrie in Goodrich.

Monmouthshire is the foodie capital of Wales, with award-winning producers and places to eat very close to the Walk. Five minutes off the path at Whitebrook is The Whitebrook, a Michelin starred restaurant where dishes are made using locally sourced food flavoured with freshly foraged herbs and plants from the valley. Silver Circle Distillery is a working distillery where you can try their Wye Valley Gin and craft spirits. They are a 3km detour off the route at Penallt. Five minutes off the path, just before Brockweir, is Kingstone Brewery, a four-barrel micro-brewery producing beers named Abbey, Tewric's Tipple and Humpty's Fuddle. Look out for Brooke's Wye Valley Dairy Company produce on local menus and in local shops. Family run, they make artisan ice cream, sorbets and soft cheeses from their pedigree Jersey cows in the Angidy Valley at Tintern. Their Welsh Gold ice cream is legendary! Parva Farm Vineyard, a stone's throw off the walk in Tintern, offers tours and tastings of their south facing vineyard.

You may also spot Wye Valley Apiaries' bee hives along the Walk as they site their bees all the way down the Wye, on heather moors in the north, in Herefordshire orchards and in ancient woodland in the south, where lime trees can give the honey an amazing taste and fragrance.

PLANNING DAY BY DAY

Follow the leaping salmon waymarkers

USING THIS GUIDE

Planning a 222km walk can be daunting but in this guide you will find all the information you need to prepare for your walk. The walk is divided into 17 stages, which vary in length from 7.7km to 19.6km, so you can choose how far you walk each day. Walking an average of 22km a day it will take you 10 days to complete. 12 days will allow you time to explore at a leisurely way as there is much to discover along the way. A faster pace of 32km a day will take seven days.

The Wye Valley Walk is one of the most rural walks you can take, but villages, market towns and a small city, located at welcome intervals along the way, mean you should be able to find places to stay, eat and explore to match your daily mileage, if you book well in advance. Factor in time for distractions, both planned and serendipitous. There is so much of interest along the path you don't want to feel you have to rush. Hay-on-Wye and Hereford alone can happily provide a day's distraction (whether to rest tired feet or escape inclement weather) so plan a rest day. Go with the flow at a pace you feel comfortable with. Peaceful places are hard to tear yourself away from – take time to stand and stare.

GPX tracks

GPX tracks for the routes in this guidebook are available to download free at www.cicerone.co.uk/1198/GPX. If you have not bought the book through the Cicerone website, or have bought the book without opening an account, please register your purchase in your Cicerone library to access GPX and update information.

A GPS device is an excellent aid to navigation, but you should also carry a map and compass and know how to use them. GPX files are provided in good faith, but in view of the profusion of formats and devices, neither the author nor the publisher accepts responsibility for their use. We provide files in a single standard GPX format that works on most devices and systems, but you may need to convert files to your preferred format using a GPX converter such as gpsvisualizer.com or one of the many other apps and online converters available.

MAPS

Although the route is waymarked you should carry a map. This guidebook includes Ordnance Survey map extracts showing a narrow corridor either side of the official route. If you prefer the real thing, which allows you to see things further off the route, these are the relevant Ordnance Survey 1:25,000 scale maps:

- Explorer 214 – Llanidloes & Newtown
- Explorer 200 – Llandrindod Wells & Elan Valley
- Explorer 188 – Builth Wells
- Explorer OL13 – Brecon Beacons National Park (Eastern Area)
- Explorer 201 – Knighton & Presteigne
- Explorer 202 – Leominster & Bromyard
- Explorer 189 – Hereford and Ross-on-Wye
- Explorer OL14 – Wye Valley & Forest of Dean

Alternatively, you can download the OS Maps app which also allows you to see where you actually are on the map, which can be very useful in bad weather on high ground.

WAYMARKING

The Wye Valley Walk is marked on the ground by 'leaping salmon' discs or stickers, and waymark arrows to show the route in both directions, usually attached to signposts, gates or stiles and sometimes trees. In urban areas they are more likely to be smaller stickers attached to existing street furniture, for example on the reverse of street signs, on telephone poles and metal signpost legs. They are being continually replaced and upgraded, but if signs are missing or prove confusing, please use the Report a Problem facility: www.wyevalley walk.org/report-a-problem. In a few locations alternative route options may be signed, for example high level routes on sections prone to flooding.

THE RIGHTS OF WAY NETWORK

The UK has a unique network of public rights of way, which are marked

THE WYE VALLEY WALK

Climbing out of Tintern to Black Cliff Wood (Stage 17)

on Ordnance Survey maps. Along the Wye Valley Walk you will see different waymarkers pointing to these other rights of way, which you can use to find places to eat and drink, reach accommodation and discover points of interest off the main Wye Valley Walk. Most of the Wye Valley Walk follows official public rights of way, which give walkers a right of passage, but don't allow them to wander off the path. There are also permissive sections of path where owners have agreed for them to be used. The Countryside and Rights of Way Act 2000 gives the public the 'right to roam' on mapped areas of 'open country'. 'Open country' means mountain, moorland, heathland, downland and registered commons and includes a large part of Plynlimon.

You may only cycle on stretches of the walk that are marked as bridleways on OS maps. Most of the walk is on public footpaths, where bicycles and horses are not allowed without permission of the landowner.

WALKING WITH DOGS

If you're walking with a dog, remember they should follow the path and not be allowed to wander. It's an offence to allow a dog to attack, worry or chase livestock so it's best to keep your dog on a lead through fields of sheep or cows or approaching farmyards. You will encounter sheep, cattle and horses on much of the Wye Valley Walk as it crosses many miles of agricultural land. Much work has been done to replace stiles with gates,

The Countryside Code

Follow advice and local signs
The arrows show the legal and recorded rights of way for different user groups

Footpath

Bridleway

Restricted Byway

Byway open to all traffic

Permissive Path
Follow advice on local signs as landowners voluntarily provide access to these paths and choose who can use them. Some open access areas are also made available in the same way.

National Trail
National Trails are created for walking, with horse-riding and cycling possible on some trails or trail sections.
www.nationaltrail.co.uk

Open Access
You can walk and explore away from paths.

www.naturalresources.wales
www.openaccess.naturalengland.org.uk

For further information visit www.countryside-code.org.uk

The Wye Valley Walk

but you may have to cross a few stiles and not all will be accessible for dogs, so be prepared to carry them over the odd one or two.

Remember these dos and don'ts:

- Do move quietly and calmly, keep your dog on a short lead, and try and walk around livestock, rather than through the middle of a herd, even if this means deviating from the path.
- Do leave gates as you found them.
- Don't hang on to your dog if threatened by livestock (usually cattle). Let it go.
- Don't get between a cow and her calf.
- Don't panic. Most cows and horses will stop before they reach you. If, as they often do, they follow out of curiosity, just walk on quietly.

PHONES AND EMERGENCIES

For police, fire, ambulance and mountain rescue dial 999 or 112. Be aware that parts of the Wye Valley Walk do not have any mobile phone reception and some areas may have only patchy coverage, particularly in valley bottoms, dense woodland and on some high upland areas. Public phone boxes have largely disappeared, but may still appear on OS maps, often being used as mini libraries or info points!

WYE VALLEY WALK PASSPORT

Walking the length of the Wye Valley Walk is a fantastic achievement. You can mark the miles by keeping a record of your journey, collecting (digital) passport stamps along the way as you finish each section, not just when you cross the border between Wales and England. When you have completed the walk claim your official Wye Valley Walk Certificate and Badge. Sign up at www.wyevalley-walk.org/passport.

How it works

At the end of each stage you will find a sign where you can scan a QR code, which will show you have completed that section of the Walk. Simply use your phone's camera to scan the QR code and your digital passport will be automatically stamped. You will find signs in the windows and doors of local shops, cafés, pubs, B&Bs, tourist attractions and tourist information centres. A few are to be found on church noticeboards. They are all accessible at any time, so you don't need to worry about arriving after hours. There are 17 stamps to collect in total and you will need at least 12 to claim your badge and certificate. Phone coverage does vary by network and weather conditions in rural areas, so if you find there is no signal take a photo of the QR code and upload when you next have signal to claim your stamp for that stage of the walk. See Appendix C for stamping locations.

Moody evening light over Gilfach Nature Reserve (Stage 2)

Old passport scheme

Badges and certificate will continue to be issued to people who have been collecting the old physical passport stamps, but please be aware that many passport stamping locations closed during the Covid pandemic and are no longer operating. If you can, take a photo and attach it with your passport application, but don't worry if you have gaps, badges and certificates will still be issued.

REPORT A PROBLEM

Maintaining 222km of footpaths is a huge task relying on walkers to help by reporting any problems they find on the ground. The Wye Valley Walk passes through four counties (Powys, Herefordshire, Gloucestershire and Monmouthshire) and two countries, which can make it confusing to report an issue. Each local authority is responsible for maintaining public rights of way in their area so please report issues to the relevant public rights of way team. See Appendix D for contacts.

THE WYE VALLEY WALK

The infant River Severn (Stage 1)

PROLOGUE
Reaching the start of the walk

Start	Opposite Market Hall, Short Bridge Street, Llanidloes SN 955 844
Finish	Rhyd-y-benwch, Hafren Forest SN 857 869
Distance	13km (8 miles)
Time	3hr 45min
Ascent	335m (1100ft)
OS map	Explorer 214 Llanidloes & Newtown
Refreshments	None on route
Public toilets	Rhyd-y-benwch
Public transport	National Express bus service 409 from London to Birmingham and Aberystwyth passes through Llanidloes (Gro car park) and Llangurig (Post Office) only at specified stops, book in advance, one bus daily. Llandrindod Wells to Aberystwyth bus service X47 stops at Llanidloes (except Sundays and public holidays). Bus service B58 runs from Rhayader to Llanidloes twice daily Monday to Friday. X75 bus service between Shrewsbury, Newtown and Caersws (nearest train station to Llanidloes) and Rhayader stops at Llanidloes (not Sundays). The nearest railway station is Caersws, a 20-minute bus ride to Llanidloes. Local taxi companies offering drop off at Rhyd-y-benwch include Llani Cars (tel 07495 306840)

The Wye Valley Walk starts at the remote location of Rhyd-y-benwch in Hafren Forest, which is 13km from Llanidloes, the nearest town. There is no public transport between Llanidloes and Rhyd-y-benwch so you have two options: arrange a drop off at Rhyd-y-benwch by friends, family or a local taxi company based in Llanidloes; alternatively, arrive on foot by taking the Severn Way from Llanidloes, a 13km waymarked route along minor country lanes, following the River Severn upstream through Old Hall to Rhyd-y-benwch. The only facilities at Rhyd-y-benwch are toilets. There is no mobile phone signal. Llanidloes is well served by buses which connect with the nearest railway stations at Caersws and Newtown.

The Wye Valley Walk

Note: It is possible to combine this Prologue section of 13km with the first half of Stage 1, a distance of 9.7km, to finish the first day's walk at Pont Rhydgaled. Time

PROLOGUE

your walk to coincide with the bus from Aberystwyth to Llangurig (you will have to hail it), where there is a pub, shop and accommodation.

STAGE 1
Rhyd-y benwch to Llangurig

Start	Rhyd-y benwch (Hafren Forest car park), Llanidloes SN 857 869
Finish	Llangurig Bridge SN 908 796
Distance	19.6km (12¼ miles)
Time	5hr 45min
Ascent	405m (1330ft)
Terrain	Forest tracks from Rhyd-y-benwch through Hafren Forest; stone track from highest point at 479m to Pont Rhydgaled; woodland, open hill and farmland to Llangurig
OS map	Explorer 214 Llanidloes & Newtown
Refreshments	None on route. Make sure you have enough food and drink for the first day of walking before you leave Llanidloes as there are no refreshments until you reach Llangurig at the end of this stage. Llangurig Post Office and Stores (closed Wednesdays and Sundays); Bluebell Inn, Llangurig
Public toilets	Rhyd-y-benwch
Public transport	National Express service 409 from Aberystwyth to Birmingham and London passes through Llangurig (Black Lion/Post Office) and Llanidloes (Gro car park) daily, only specified stops, book in advance. Bus service X49 Aberystwyth to Llandrindod Wells stops in Llanidloes and Llangurig (not Sundays or public holidays). Bus service X79 between Llangurig and Rhayader stops in Llangurig and Llanidloes (not Sundays or public holidays)

This section starts beside the River Severn and runs alongside mountain streams before climbing up through pine forest to open moorland with extensive views across the Cambrian Mountains. A gravel track descends all the way from the watershed down to the A44, through a landscape dotted with industrial archaeology. Motor rallying events take place at Sweet Lamb and in Hafren Forest so check for path closures before setting out. The second half of this stage is along quiet forest tracks, through riverside fields, with a final steep climb up to Llwyn-gwyn (400m) before descending to Llangurig.

STAGE 1 – RHYD-Y BENWCH TO LLANGURIG

Note: If you are collecting passport stamps before you leave Rhyd-y-benwch take your photo beside the information board or scan the QR code on the 'All Walks' sign and collect your digital passport stamp when you have mobile signal later in the day.

Rhyd-y-benwch to Pont Rhydgaled (9.7km, 2hr 5min)

Follow the 'All Walks' path downhill to meet the River Severn. Turn right along the boardwalk. Follow the gravel track uphill past the decked seating area, through the mossy woodland full of ferns and foxgloves in season, keeping left at the junction of paths to follow the river on your left. Pass a timber picnic shelter and follow the path round to the right and then cross the 'Severn Bridge'. ▶

The streams here are stained bright orange, a sign of having flowed through copper-bearing strata.

This tiny stream is the **River Severn** and the next time you see it will be near journey's end, where views from the Eagle's Nest take in the mighty River Severn and the two Severn bridges. The Severn Way is the longest riverside walk in Britain: 338km from its source on Plynlimon to the mouth of the Severn at Bristol.

Planted by the Forestry Commission in the 1930s, **Hafren Forest** takes its name from the Welsh name for the River Severn, Afon Hafren, which rises in a deep blanket bog, high on the slopes of Plynlimon.

The Cambrian Mountains (photo: Adam Fisher)

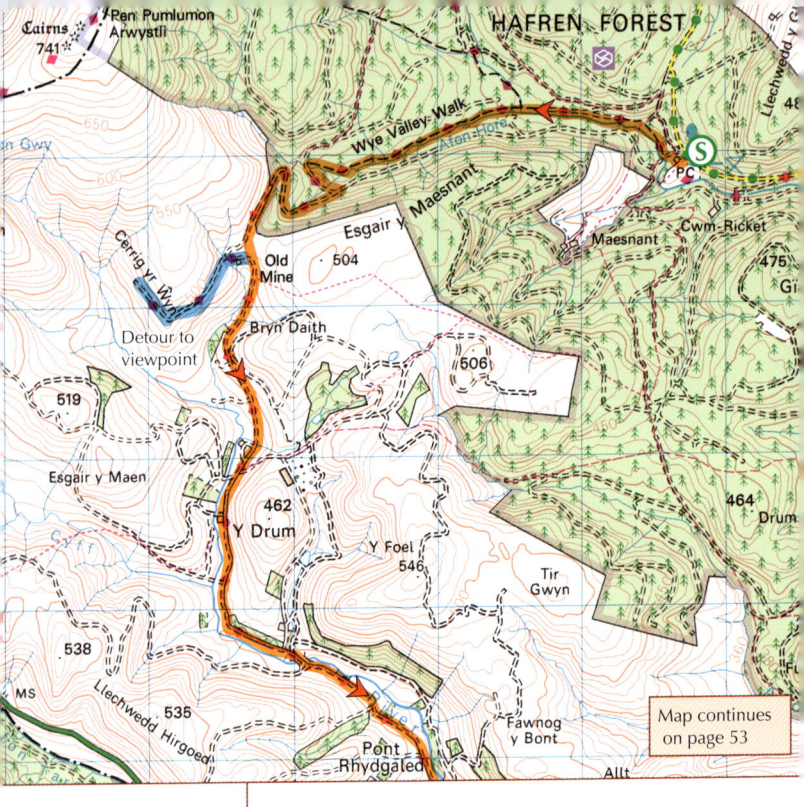

Turn left signed Wye Valley Walk. Follow the track beside the stream, the **Afon Hore** (*afon* is the Welsh word for river), ignoring bridge and gates to either side. The path soon starts to gently climb, then more steeply along a shale path, as the stream beside you bubbles over boulders. ◀ As you climb you will catch glimpses of the brooding moorland slopes of Plynlimon. Reaching a wide forest track turn left over the bridge, where the Afon Hore forms a small waterfall. Take the first forest track on your right, which winds uphill along a series of wide bends.

Eventually you emerge from the forest and go through a metal gate (SN828 868). Continue on a gravel road which soon reaches a high point of 479m, where the view opens out below. Stay on the gravel road as it curves downhill.

Look out for bilberries in summer and lichens and mosses throughout the year.

STAGE 1 – RHYD-Y BENWCH TO LLANGURIG

INDUSTRIAL HERITAGE IN THE MOUNTAINS

Mining for silver and lead was a major industry in this area during the 18th and 19th centuries, although there is evidence that lead was mined in the Middle Ages, and even earlier. In this valley there were at least four mines working mainly for lead, although the Nant-yr-Eira Mine also produced copper. The remains of Nant-yr-Eira Mine are hidden in the woods down to the right of the track. In the late 19th century some 33 tonnes of lead were recovered from old Bronze Age open cut mine workings, shafts and levels here. With many old mine shafts in the valley please keep to the track.

The main gravel track continues downhill passing, on the right, the site of the **Nat Iago Lead Mine**. ▶

A signed path on the right leads to a viewpoint to the source of the Wye

The **Nat Iago Lead Mine** operated from 1846 to 1917 and you can still see evidence of spoil heaps, processing buildings and machinery, along with tracks and tramways from the various adits (tunnels into the hill) leading downhill to the crushers. Power was supplied by a Pelton wheel, a metal wheel with cups instead of paddles, operated by high-pressure water brought down the hillside from reservoirs. The shafts and levels are dangerous so don't go exploring.

A mountain bouquet of heather, bilberries and lichen

Over the watershed and looking to the west

Go through a gate beside a small plantation. Soon after, at the junction of tracks, keep right downhill. At the next Wye Valley Walk signpost you catch your first glimpse of the Wye to your right, where a gauge hut straddles the tiny stream, monitoring the flow of the Wye. Other weather statistics are collected nearby.

PUMLUMON (PLYNLIMON) AND THE SOURCE OF THE WYE

Three rivers have their source on Plynlimon (Pumlumon in Welsh): the Severn, the Rheidol and the Wye. If you would like to get a little closer to the source of the Wye, the first signposted path on the right (5km from the start of Stage 1) (SN 825 863) leads to a superb viewpoint looking towards the source (which is another 2km north west at SN 802 871). The land to the source of the Wye is open access land under the Countryside and Rights of Way Act 2000 for England and Wales and is open for the public to walk over. However, it is boggy, uneven and not waymarked, so should only be attempted by well-equipped, experienced walkers. Plynlimon is the highest point in the Cambrian Mountains. It is one of the most important upland areas for nature conservation in Wales, with blanket bog, acid grassland and dwarf shrub heath.

Plynlimon has been an open air laboratory for studying the environment for the last 50 years since the UK Centre for Ecology & Hydrology launched an ambitious project to examine the effect on water courses of planting forests in upland areas, in contrast to keeping moorland farmland. The in-depth knowledge of the Plynlimon catchment which has been gathered over the last half century will provide valuable data for climate change mitigation.

Stage 1 – Rhyd-y benwch to Llangurig

Continue on the main gravel road, through a gate passing the Sweet Lamb Motorsport Complex (SN827850) to your right.

> This was the site of the **Wye Valley Lead Mines** that worked between 1846 and 1880. Most of the mine features have been destroyed by the construction of the Sweet Lamb Motorsport Complex, but on the right, in the stream bed, evidence can be seen of industrial activity and construction. Another mine, the West Wye Valley Mine, lies on the hillside to the west, which operated during the same period producing lead and zinc. The motorsport complex has 20 miles of gravel and tarmac road stages used for testing rally cars and off-road vehicles and for adventure bike training. It is often used as a film location and also holds major events, which could impact on your enjoyment of this part of the walk.

Keep straight on, ignoring the bridge to the right. Further on walk to the left of the stock sheds. Ignore road to the right and after 1.3km cross Pont Cefn-brwŷn, a small bridge over the Wye. Continue on the farm track with the river to your left, ignoring any tracks off to left or right. The track becomes tarmac as you pass through the farmyard and motorcycle training facility buildings to reach the A44 at **Pont Rhydgaled**.

It is possible to hail the X47 bus between Aberystwyth and Llangurig at Pont Rhydgaled for a 7min ride to Llanguirg, where there is a shop, pub and accommodation.

Pont Rhydgaled to Hendre (3.7km, 1hr)

Cross the A44, turn left and immediately right (signposted Wye Valley Walk), crossing the Afon Tarrenig just before it flows into the Wye. Soon after the bridge turn left to walk for 20 minutes along a level forestry track until you reach a gate on the left (SN 851 821). ▶ Go through the gate and bear right on the track. Before you reach the riverbank, keep right of the fir trees (to avoid marshy area) and join the flood bank further along. Turn right

> If river levels are too high here, take the alternate high level route through woodland, marked in blue on the map.

through the gate into a meadow, ignoring the footbridge over the Wye, and keep left to follow the field boundary. Go through a double set of gates over a stream. Continue along the field boundary to the corner of the field and cross a small bridge over a stream. Turn left and go through a gate, turning right to walk along a tree-lined riverbank. Go through another gate into a field and keep left along the riverbank. As the river curves to the right keep to the left of the old fence line, heading for a gate on the right in the distance. Go through this gate and walk straight ahead towards a nearby waymarker.

Turn left and walk uphill to a waymarker post to the left of the field. Keep on the same line uphill heading for a gateway with waymarker. Go through the gateway (may be muddy) and keep left along a boggy section heading for another waymarker. Continue across the field following the contour line to the waymarker beside a tree. Head across the next field on the same contour. You will soon see a red bridge over the Wye in the distance. Aim for the gap in the hedge and keep going on the same line across a boggy patch and a small stream. Nearing the bridge head for a pedestrian gate. Go through the gate, over a small bridge and follow the fence down to the track in front of the farmhouse at Hendre (leave route here, turning left, for the footpath to accommodation near Penlon).

Hendre to Glangwy (3.4km, 1hr)

Turn left and walk down to the river behind the wooden cabin and lake. At the river turn right heading for a gateway. Go through the gate and bear right, away from the river, heading for a tall waymarker sign. Turn left at the sign and follow the track to a gateway, heading uphill, away from the river. Pass a tumbledown farm building on the right. Continue climbing. Where the track levels out turn left downhill. Keep on this track, which crosses a stream and curves around **Ty-mawr Farm.** (To reach the B&B at Plas Bwlch, leave the route here, taking the footpath to the left over the bridge and keeping right to head up to the A470 at Plas Bwlch.) At the weak bridge sign on the left, keep straight on through the farmyard, keeping to

Stage 1 – Rhyd-y benwch to Llangurig

the left to go through a gateway into the field. Continue along the riverbank, through fields on a stony track with the river just to your left, until you reach the second gate where the track leaves the river, veering rightish. Keep to the right of the fence line on the stony track, taking a short cut as the river meanders left. At a large ash tree follow the path to the left of the tree to go through a gate. Head straight across the field and go through another gate to rejoin the riverside path.

Cross a tiny stream and keep straight on beside the Wye. At the waymarker bear diagonally right towards a metal gate. Go through the gate, cross the bridge and follow the fence uphill to a gate on the right. Go through the gate into a wood and turn left. Follow the path around to the left and uphill to a tall signpost. This area

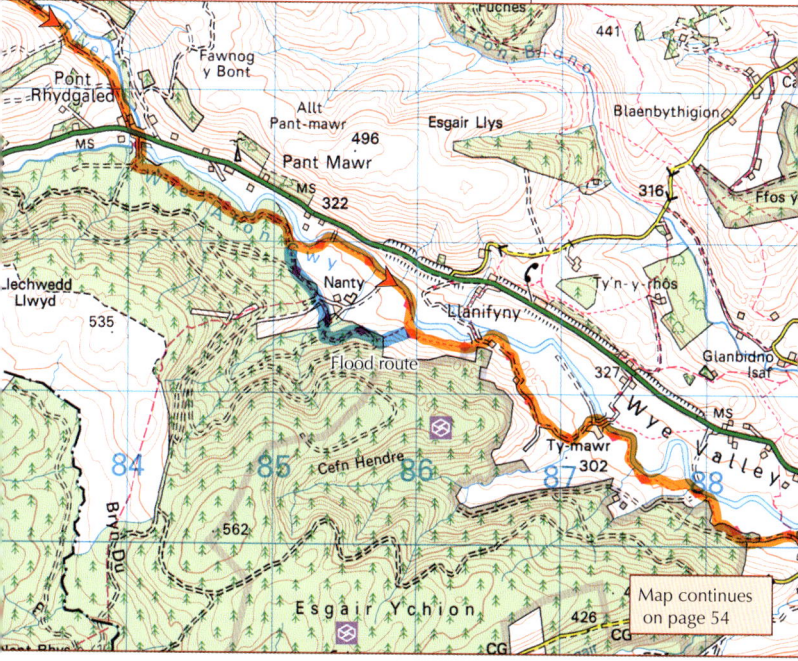

The Wye Valley Walk

of recently cleared forest is liable to be overgrown with bracken in summer. Come out on a wide forest track and turn left. Keep on, passing through a gate beside a cattle grid. Go through another gate to pass Pen-y-geulan to your left and turn right immediately down the lane. Cross the cattle grid and turn left down a tarmac lane. At the T-junction turn right at **Glangwy**. (To reach Glangwy Farm Campsite, turn left here.)

Glangwy to Llangurig (3.2km, 1hr)

Keep on this lane, ignoring track to left, past **Troed-yr-esgair**. After Pen y Rhos cottage on the right go through a metal gate and keep straight on. Go through another gate and turn left straight away, over a stile and follow the fence on the left uphill, until reaching a stile on the left. Go over the stile and head diagonally right up hill across the field heading for a waymarker. Follow the waymarker to walk along the top of the old hedgerow bank and over a stile heading for another gate. Turn right before the gate and walk uphill to another stile. Go over the stile and turn left. Follow the fence uphill and just before the fir plantation ends the path turns right steeply uphill. Follow the fence line through a gate.

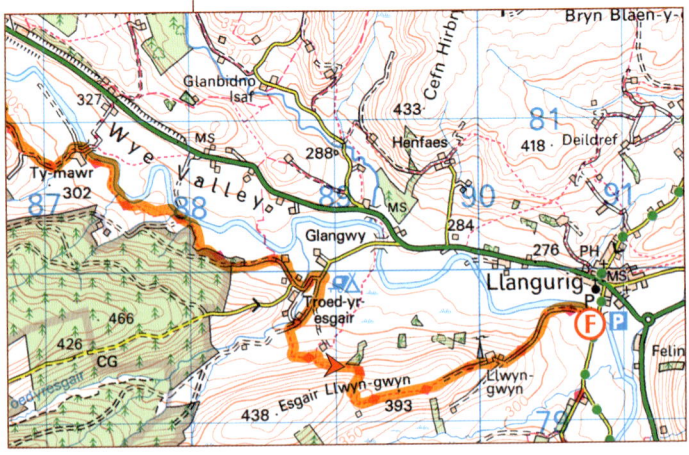

STAGE 1 – RHYD-Y BENWCH TO LLANGURIG

The path curves slightly to the right, but still mirroring the fence line, staying high to avoid boggy ground. Then turn left aiming for the gate in the corner of the field. (Note: gate is not in the location shown on the OS map.) Go through the gate and walk along the right-hand fence line a short distance to pick up a small track, curving to the left below the summit. Mirror the hedge line on the right, soon passing a gateway. Follow the sheep track along the same contour line. There is a bank to your right which may be obscured by bracken in summer. Keep to the left of the bank and fence posts, eventually spotting two telecoms towers. Head straight for them as the path descends, goes through a gateway (SN 899 793) and passes to the right of them. Go through a gate into **Llwyn-gwyn** farmyard, around the pond and follow the track round to the right. Turn left onto a tarmac lane heading down to **Llangurig**, which you can now see in front of you. ▶ At the main road, turn left over Pont Llangurig, the end of this stage, for services in the village and to pick up your passport stamp at Llangurig Post Office & Stores.

St Curig's Church, Llangurig

St Curig's Church comes into view as you meet the Wye.

St Curig's Church Llangurig has been a holy place since the Age of the Saints when St Curig founded a monastery in the 6th century on the site of the present-day church. After the Normans arrived, Llangurig found itself connected to two Cistercian monasteries, Abbey Cwm Hir and Strata Florida. The Normans, who didn't recognise Celtic saints, changed the church's dedication to Cyricus the Martyr. Built around 1350, the tower is the oldest remaining part of the church. A rood screen and loft were added in the 15th century. The church standing today was inspired by the romanticism of the late 19th century. Sir Gilbert Scott, the great Victorian church rebuilder, remodelled the church in 1878, installing a copy of the original rood screen and commissioning stained glass windows by Burlison and Grylls depicting religious subjects, Welsh history and the local Clochfaen family heraldry.

LLANGURIG

Llangurig is the first village on the Wye as it flows south from the slopes of Plynlimon. A small settlement, it has a pub, post office and shop (closed Wednesdays and Sundays), and a few places to stay. There is an interesting water feature on the main road opposite St Curig's Church, remembering Colonel Hope Lloyd-Verney, who gave the first water supply to the village in 1888. A 3km walk from Llangurig will take you to Glan-y-rhyd, a small cottage overlooking Marsh's Pool. The artist and naturalist Robert Gibbings lived here for a short time in the 1940s while he researched *Coming Down the Wye*, a beautiful book illustrated with his wood engravings that did much to popularise natural history.

STAGE 2

Llangurig to Rhayader

Start	Llangurig Bridge SN 908 796
Finish	Clocktower at Rhayader crossroads SN 970 680
Distance	19.4km (12 miles)
Time	6hr 45min
Ascent	535m (1755ft)
Terrain	Open hillside and upland moorland; woodland; three sections of minor road
OS map	Explorers 200 Landrindod Wells & Elan Valley, 214 Llanidloes and Newtown
Refreshments	None on route so make sure to stock up before leaving Llangurig
Public toilets	Gilfach Nature Reserve Centre (when open), Rhayader car park
Public transport	X47 bus service between Llangurig and Rhayader (except Sundays and public holidays)

This has to be one of the most spectacular stages, venturing into the uplands of Mid Wales and reaching the highest point on the Wye Valley Walk at 480m (1,575ft). The first section is uphill all the way to Nantyhendy Hill, with an hour or so of high-level walking over open moorland. It's a slightly gentler descent into the delightful Dernol Valley, picking up a peaceful lane following the Nant-y-Dernol as it flows down to join the Wye. A beautiful section of gated lane drops down to Gilfach Nature Reserve. A gentle walk along the Afon Marteg is followed by a steep uphill climb to Gilfach Farm. A breathtaking view over the nature reserve is the reward for an even steeper climb onto the moorland above Gilfach. Then it's across fields to reach a minor road dropping down into Rhayader, with an unexpected last-minute uphill section. From heather-clad hill tops to sheltered stands of sessile oaks this stage has got it all!

Be prepared for wind, rain, hail and snow on the high section over Nant-yr-hendy Hill. If a lower-level route is preferred the quiet minor road to the west of the River Wye can be followed all the way from Llangurig to Rhayader.

THE WYE VALLEY WALK

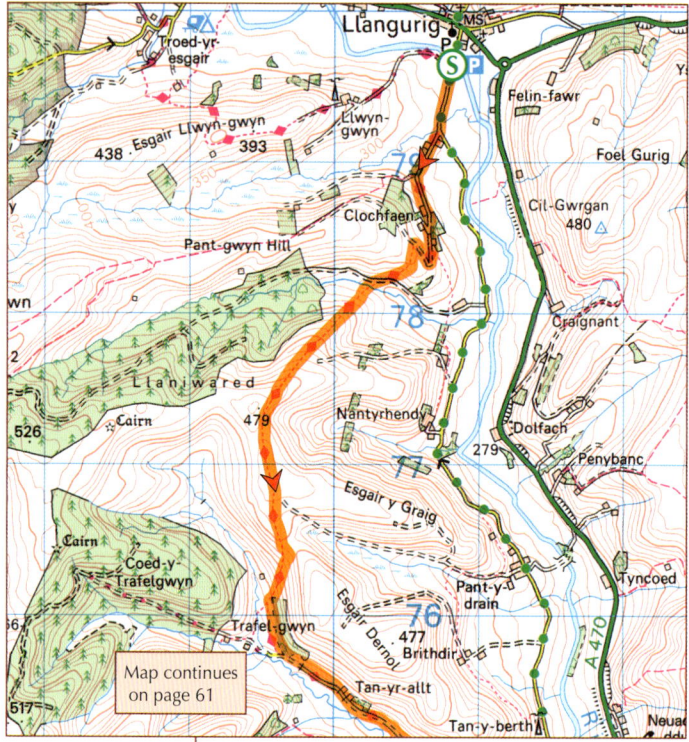

Note: There are many 'gated' sections along the rural lanes on this stage, so be ready to open and close gates, leaving them as you found them.

Llangurig to summit of Nant-yr-hendy Hill (3.3km, 1hr 40min)

From Llangurig Bridge walk away from the village along the minor road. When the road forks bear right and stay on the road as it gradually climbs uphill, passing an attractive black and white house called **Clochfaen** on your right.

Clochfaen is a rare example in Wales of an Arts and Crafts house designed by WAS Benson, a leading figure in the Arts and Crafts movement and a colleague of William Morris. This striking, half-timbered house was the work of Sir Harry Lloyd Verney, who inherited the Clochfaen estate in 1913. He set about upgrading a modest house to an 11-bedroom mansion. Following the traditions of the Arts and Crafts movement, building materials came from local sources, using stone from the estate quarry, oak timbers from the original house and sand from the Wye. Harry had been gentleman usher and deputy master of the household of King Edward VII and later groom-in-waiting to King George V. In 1917 a manned sentry box was installed outside the main house when Prince Albert (who later became King George VI) came to recuperate after serving in the Battle of Jutland. Clochfaen has subsequently been a hotel, school and grand holiday home, and now offers B&B and self-catering accommodation to visitors.

Clochfaen – an Arts and Crafts house

Where the lane bears sharp right keep straight on between two large metal pillars and through a gate. The view opens out as you follow the farm track uphill, then sharp right and up to a gateway. Turn sharp left to walk alongside the hedge. Go through the gate and head diagonally right downhill towards a gate. You can just about make out a gravel track from the top, which the gate leads onto. Go through the gate, cross the gravel track and immediately turn left down a path to a stream.

Cross the bridge over the Nant y Clochfaen and immediately turn off the gravel track, heading uphill alongside a boggy ditch to the right, to reach a gate. Go through the gate and bear left, climbing steeply and aiming for a pedestrian gate in the fence line above. Go through the gate and continue walking straight uphill, heading for another gateway in the middle of the field, which soon comes into view. Bear right after the gateway heading diagonally across the field to a Wye Valley Walk signpost on the fence line at the top of the field, which will be visible nearer the top. Go through the gate and head slightly right to a tall waymarker. At this waymarker post follow the arrow to the right. You should be able to make out more tall posts showing the route over the moorland. At the next post, look for another tall waymarker on higher ground slightly to the right, which you reach by making your way across reedy, boggy ground. At the third marker post you are very close to the summit of Nan-ty-hendy Hill.

> At 480m, **Nant-yr-hendy Hill** is the highest point on the Wye Valley Walk, so if it's not too windy and the visibility is good it's worth turning right for a few paces to reach the top for the 360-degree view.

Nant-yr-hendy Hill to Pont Marteg (9.6km, 2hr 50min)
Standing by the waymarker, get your bearings and head left (south) through the reedy tussocks to a stile and gate. Go over the stile and walk straight ahead, across a flattish section which starts to descend gently, so you can spot the next tall waymarker and stile. Go over the stile and head slightly left to the next tall waymarker. Keep

heading downhill in the same diagonal (southerly) direction, eventually reaching the fence line on your right near the corner of the field. Continue to the corner (there may be a small livestock pen before the gates at some times of year) and turn right downhill between the gates, following a fenced farm track. Go through the gate and continue steeply downhill at Blaen-y-cwm.

Go through another gate and keep straight on for a short distance until you meet a grassy track. Turn left. When you reach the tarmac road, turn left. Pass **Tan-yr-allt** (gates may be closed on this lane section). Stay on the road, crossing two cattle grids, with a lovely stream flowing to your right. At the road junction keep straight on (right), continuing until reaching another T-junction, just before a bridge. Turn right here and, soon after, left. The Wye now flows beside the road for a short distance. Stay on this road, which is lined in places with unusual stone slab fences typical to this area, for about 3km, passing **Graig Safn-y-coed** and **Glyn Gwy**. You may have to open and close gates. ▶

In late summer the hilltops to the left are clad with purple heather.

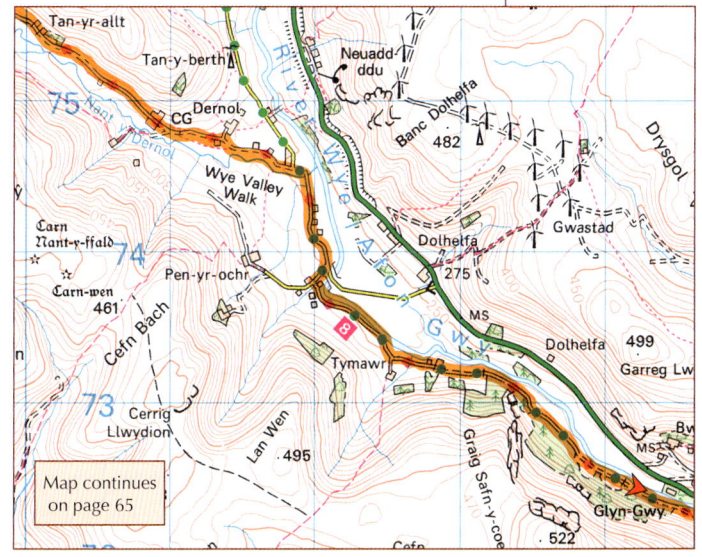

Stone slab fences are an unusual feature below Safn-y-coed

Around 2km after Safn-y-coed look out for a bench under a tree on the right and soon afterwards a waymarker on the left, where you leave the road, taking the footpath downhill on a grassy path which weaves through woodland trees and over rocky outcrops. Go through the gate and follow the path round to the right across the field, where there are remnants of stone slab walls. Look out for a waymarker just after the ruined wall and bear left, following a sheep track around the contour line. When you can see a gate in the fence below to the left, head down to the gate. Go through the gate into a lovely stand of oak and birch trees and down to the bridge to cross the Wye. Follow the path up to the A470 at **Pont Marteg** and bear right across the carpark to cross the road at the entrance to Gilfach Nature Reserve.

It is possible to hail buses on the A470 to Rhayader, where there is a good selection of services and accommodation.

STAGE 2 – LLANGURIG TO RHAYADER

Note: Your OS map may show the old route of the Wye Valley Walk running to the south of the river Marteg. The official route stays on the north side of the river.

Pont Marteg to Rhayader (6.5km, 2hr 15min)

Walk up the road to a small structure on the right that offers a sheltered place for a picnic or coffee break if it's wet. Follow the path to the right of the road along the nature trail, passing an old railway bridge on the right. After a while come to a bench and turn right downhill and through a gate to reach the Afon Marteg. ▶ Pass the waterfall viewing platform on the right, which is a great place to watch salmon leaping in autumn, and the remains of a railway viaduct on the left. At the gate turn right over the bridge, passing the dipper hide, which is a wonderful place to view these birds. Follow the tarmac uphill steeply to Gilfach farm. There is a bench half-way if you want to catch your breath. Walk into the farmyard where you will find the Byre, which provides toilets, picnic benches and information about Gilfach Nature Reserve.

Look out for the 'wash pool' on the right, where sheep were herded through the water to rid them of mud and insects before their fleeces were shorn.

GILFACH NATURE RESERVE AND WELSH LONGHOUSE

Gilfach is a Site of Special Scientific Interest because of the range of habitats found here – high moorland, oak woodlands, farmland and a rocky, tumbling river with a dramatic waterfall, which supports outstanding biodiversity. Over 1300 species of plants and animals have been recorded, many of which are vulnerable and nationally rare. There are more than 400 species of lichens and over 140 species of mosses and liverworts. In summer, look out for scarce fritillary butterflies, the bloody-nosed beetle (a slow-moving black beetle often found on grassy tracks, which exudes a red fluid when alarmed) and glow-worms on the old railway track after dark.

The farmhouse at Gilfach is a Grade II* listed late medieval longhouse, built around 1550. Medieval farmstead sites, known as 'house platforms', are found all over the uplands of Wales. They were constructed by digging into the hillside and pushing the resulting soil downhill to create a terrace. They were the origin of the Welsh longhouse (*tŷ hir*), where people and animals lived under the same roof, with the family on the uphill side of the building and the livestock on the lower side so that manure drained away downhill.

The Wye Valley Walk

Walk between the longhouse and the barn up to a signpost. Go through the gate and turn right, signposted 'Rhayader 3.5 km'. Note the stone slab fence along the path. Go through the gate and follow the grassy path uphill diagonally. Close to the top, when you can see the fence line in front, the path forks gently left to a marker post, which you can't see until you are close to it. At the marker go straight ahead to go through a stile. To the left you can see a motorsports track. Follow the track downhill through a series of gates. At the final gate turn right onto the road and follow the road downhill. There is a sting in the tail to this section, with an unexpected steep uphill just when you think you should be at the end! The saving grace is that the road is lined by gorgeous oak woodland. (Glamping domes at Coed Cochion can be accessed to the left as you pass Cefn Coed wood.) When you reach the outskirts of **Rhayader**, continue to the road junction. Turn right to walk down to the town centre, passing toilets and the leisure centre on the left. At the junction turn left and walk down to the crossroads and clock tower where this stage ends.

Near Gilfach Nature Reserve (photo: Adam Fisher)

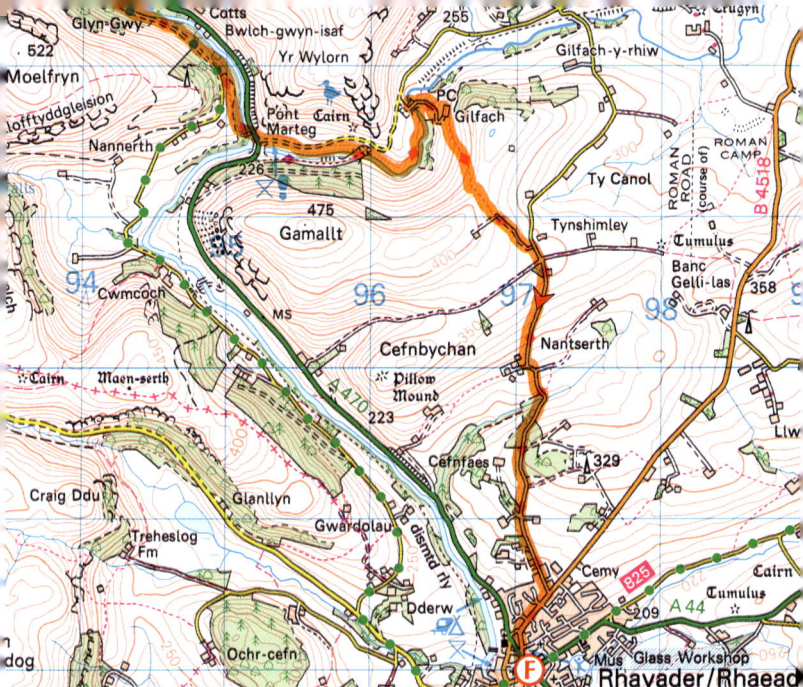

RHAYADER

Little remains of Rhayader Castle today, but it was built by the Welsh Lord of Deheubarth, Rhys ap Gruffydd, around 1178. He wanted to control the river crossing and defend this Welsh territory from the Normans, who had killed his son-in-law. As you move south you will find that it's the other way around and most castles were built by the Normans to keep the Welsh out! Rhayader is the first town on the River Wye and in recent years has become the outdoor adventure capital of Mid Wales. It's a friendly town with a good selection of independent shops and local traders along with food, drink and accommodation options. Check out what's on at the Lost ARC, a live music venue, café and gallery just off West Street, and CARAD, Rhayader's museum and community arts centre. Just outside Rhayader is Gigrin Farm, famous for its red kite feeding centre.

The Wye Valley Walk

STAGE 3

Rhayader to Newbridge

Start	Clock tower at Rhayader crossroads SN 970 680
Finish	Opposite Pen-y-bont Farm, Newbridge-on-Wye SO 012 582
Distance	15.5km (9½ miles)
Time	4hr 45min
Ascent	425m (1395ft)
Terrain	Mainly farmland and woodland, some quite steep; highest point 378m (1240ft)
OS map	Explorer 200 Llandrindod Wells & Elan Valley
Refreshments	None on route; approximately 1km off route, petrol station with shop and café at Doldowlod on A470 near Llanwrthwl
Public toilets	None on route; at petrol station on A470 near Llanwrthwl
Public transport	Bus service X47 between Llandrindod Wells and Aberystwyth stops at Llanwrthwl (at end of bridge on A470) and Newbridge-on-Wye (New Inn) (not Sundays)

This stage is a pleasant mix of farmland, open hill, woodland and old roads. Leaving Rhayader you pass the waterfall that gave the town its name. Gentle walking on minor roads and farm tracks brings you to some early excitement, a suspension bridge across the Afon Elan. A long steep climb, with excellent views, takes you up onto the open moorland of Graig Allt-y-bont, followed by a steady descent down to Llanwrthwl. A minor road leads to an old coaching track (shared with National Cycle Route 8) which runs along the base of Trembyd Hill with pleasing views across the Wye Valley. The final section is over fields to reach a quiet road leading down to the end of this stage at Newbridge-on-Wye.

Rhayader to Llanwrthwl (6.8km, 2hr 15min)

Start from the clock tower at Rhayader crossroads and walk down West Street, crossing the bridge over the Wye. Keep left for a short distance before turning left

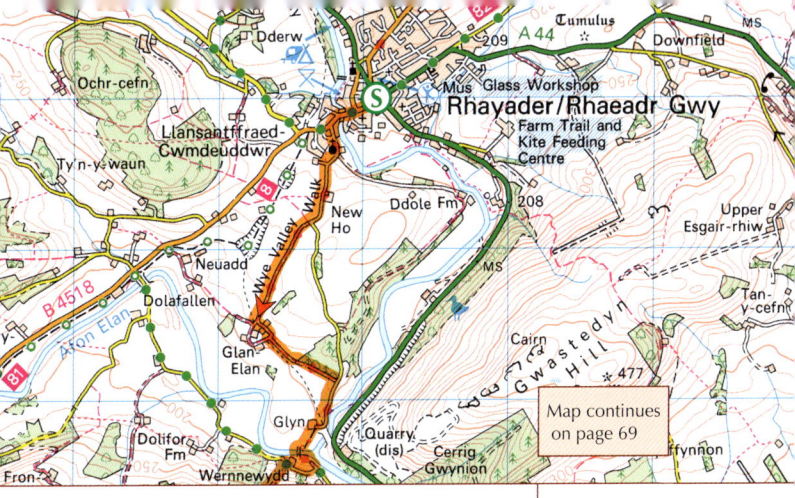

signposted 'Wye Valley Walk'. To view the waterfall, go down the steps to the left of the toilets.

> When the Wye reaches Rhayader it encounters a rocky channel and the resulting waterfall gave the town its Welsh name of **Rhaeadr Gwy**, meaning 'the waterfall of the Wye'.

You can walk across the park to the swings to exit the park, turning left onto the lane. Stay on this lane until it bears left after **New House**. The Wye Valley Walk goes straight ahead along the gravel track signposted 'WVW'. When you get to a junction of paths turn left. The old railway line crosses the track here. Follow the track through the farmyard, going between two buildings, and round to the right. Turn left just before the old railway bridge through a gateway. The route runs immediately to the left of the railway line, along a pretty track bordered by oak woods. When you reach the tarmac lane turn right and descend down to where the Wye flows on your left. Stay on the lane as it goes under what was an old railway bridge and up to a farm. Turn left in front of the barn and go through two gateways down an ancient lane. The path forks left down to an old fording point, but keep right to reach **Glyn Bridge** (SN 965 656).

Discovering the quirky **bridges** that cross the tributaries flowing into the Wye is one of the delights of the Wye Valley Walk. Glyn Bridge is a narrow suspension bridge that replaced an old fording point to the left. It is one of several similar suspension bridges in this part of the Upper Wye Valley, built in the 1960s by a local Newbridge-on-Wye company.

The Glyn suspension bridge over the Afon Elan

Cross the bridge and turn left, soon arriving at the junction of the rivers Wye and Elan, where a well-placed bench makes for a pleasant refreshment stop. Go through a gate and turn right on reaching the lane. Climb uphill and at the first house on the right, **Wernnewydd House** (SN 964 655), look out for a track on the left leading up to a gate (this can be difficult to spot from the road when summer vegetation is tall). Go through the gate and start climbing up a narrow path between two fields. Go through another gate onto open moorland, following a steep climb parallel to the fence on the right, passing a small cottage. Keep on the path, which may be invaded by bracken during summer months, following the woodland boundary to your right and after a while you will

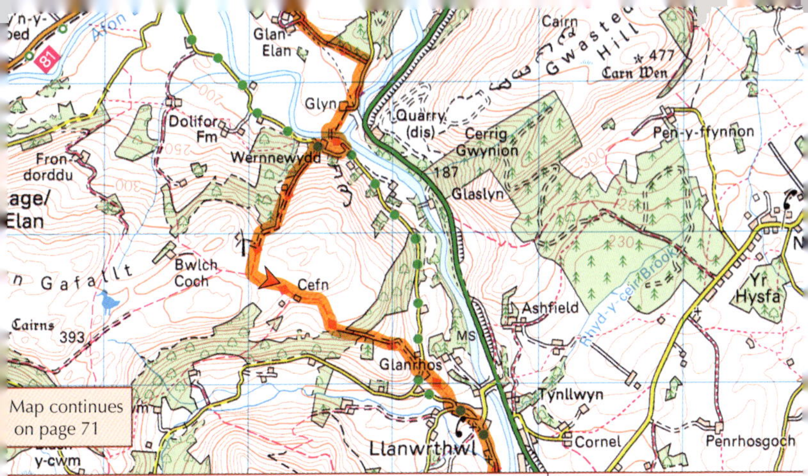

Map continues on page 71

spot a small wind turbine higher up the hill. Pass Coed Dolifor, owned by the Woodland Trust, on the right. Soon after the path levels out, passing a waymarker on the right. Continue in the same direction along the field access track, passing the turbine.

This open moorland is called **Graig Allt-y-bont** and is part of Carngafallt Nature Reserve, owned and managed by the RSPB. In summer you are most likely to see red kite, buzzard, stonechat, whinchat and redstart. During the colder months woodcock and migrant thrushes, such as fieldfare and red-wing, may be spotted.

On the climb up to Graig Allt-y-bont

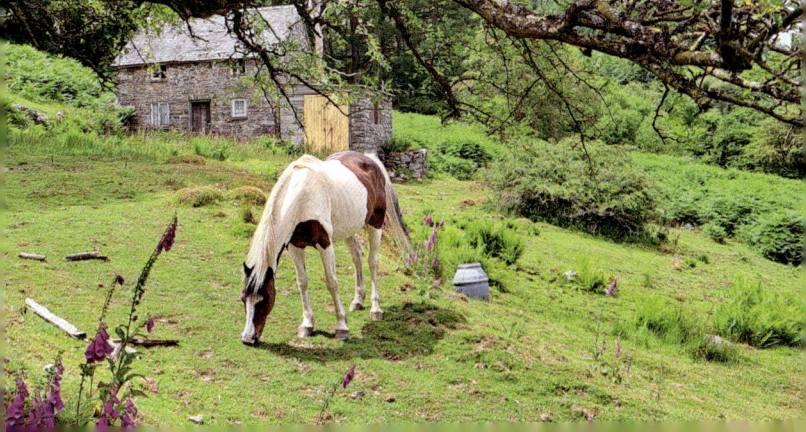

Turn left at the junction of tracks, following the main track as it curves across flat moorland. Go through a gateway and continue in the same direction, through a gated farmyard at **Cefn**. The view opens out after the second gate and the track starts descending. Stay on this track, where there may be gates to open and close, until reaching a gate that opens onto a road at Dolgai. (For camping and self-catering accommodation 0.5km off route at Doliago Farm, leave the route here and turn right along the road.) Turn left along the road and immediately turn right down a narrow path coming out onto another road. Turn left and walk into **Llanwrthwl**.

(Leave the route here to access local services at the petrol station on the A470, turning left at the church, crossing the Wye and turning right. Café, shop and Vulcan Lodge self-catering after 0.5km at Doldowlod.)

Llanwrthwl to Newbridge (8.7km, 2hr 30min)
Turn right by the church along the minor road and pass the chapel on the right. You will soon hear the sound of the Wye below you.

Trembyd is the Welsh word for 'View of the World'

STAGE 3 – RHAYADER TO NEWBRIDGE

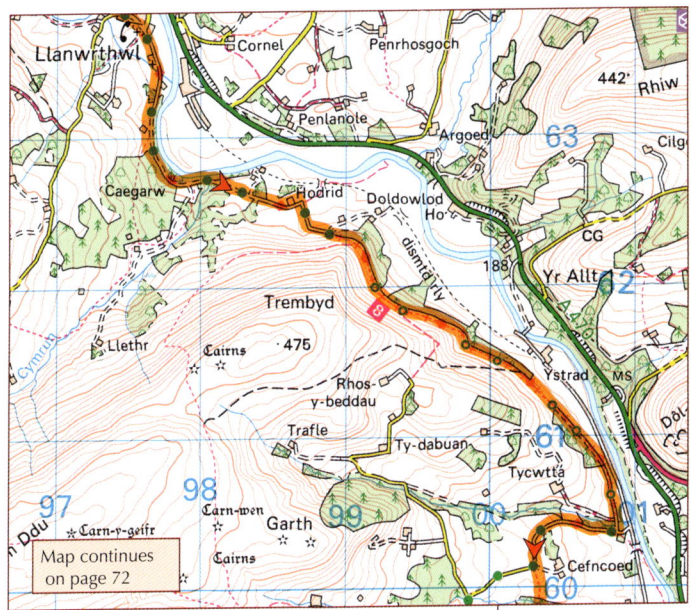

St Gwrthwl's Church was built in Victorian times but stands on a very old site. The standing stone south of the porch may have prehistoric origins. The belfry, carrying one bell, is built away from the church on the north side and is constructed of reclaimed railway sleepers.

Continue on this road, passing **Hodrid House** on the left. Where the road forks take the right fork up to, and through, a gate onto **Trembyd**.

The hill to the right is **Trembyd** which marks the eastern edge of one of the largest areas of open upland common land in Wales, with much of the land owned by the National Trust. A challenging 16km circular walk, off the Wye Valley Walk, will take you to the summit at 600m.

THE WYE VALLEY WALK

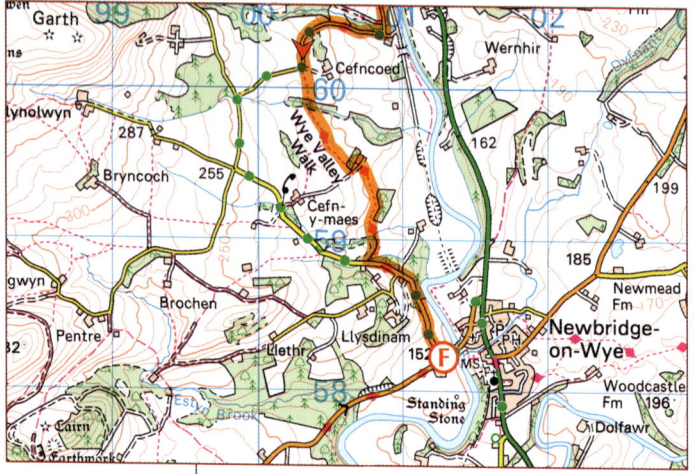

There are lovely views across the valley to the left to Doldowlod House.

The route continues along an ancient coach road, which today is also National Cycle Route 8. ◀

Doldowlod House is a Jacobean-style country house built for one of the leading industrialist families of the late 18th and early 19th century. The engineer and inventor James Watt bought the estate when he retired in 1803. His son, James Watt junior, constructed the present house in the 1840s. An extension was added by James Watt Gibson-Watt after he inherited Doldowlod in 1874.

The route continues through overhanging trees, mostly birch and cherries. Continue on the track as it leaves the National Trust land, passing through several gates. Eventually, the track meets a tarmac lane. Go left to cross a bridge and keep right along the lane signposted Newbridge-on-Wye. After 0.8km the road bears right at **Upper Cefncoed Farm** but the path goes straight ahead through a pedestrian gate into the field. Follow the hedge to your left across the field, to a gate in the far left-hand corner. Go through the gate and turn right down steps,

Stage 3 – Rhayader to Newbridge

over a wooden footbridge and up the other side to the left. At the top of the gully walk a short distance along the field edge until you can see a pedestrian gate in the fence line to the right. Go through the gate and head straight across the field towards the left-hand fence and then on to a veteran oak tree. After the second oak tree look for a pedestrian gate in the fence ahead. Go through the left-hand gate and then over a board walk. Now follow the fence to your right to the corner of the field, crossing another boardwalk on the way. Go through the gate and turn left, down the farm track to Ty'n-y-coed farm.

Turn right in front of the farm and walk to the far left-hand corner of the field. Go through an opening in the hedge and continue beside the left-hand hedge to the pedestrian gate in the corner. Continue along the left hedgerow to a gate and head straight across the field to another pedestrian gate. Cross two footbridges, and after the second footbridge walk straight ahead to follow the right-hand hedge to a pedestrian gate. Go through the gate and continue beside the fence through another gate onto a lane. Turn left, soon passing Llysdinam Gardens on the right. ▶ Stay on this lane following it down to the junction with a busy road, the B4358, where this stage ends. To collect your passport stamp and find supplies turn left and walk over the Wye Bridge up to the village of Newbridge-on-Wye.

20 acres of beautifully planted grounds and walled kitchen garden can be visited by appointment. Having been in the same family for 150 years the gardens are now run by the Llysdinam Trust: www.llysdinamgardens.org.

NEWBRIDGE

Newbridge is a small village with a post office and shop (passport stamping location), a pub and limited accommodation options. Disserth Camping is 2.5km off route at the end of Stage 3, east of Newbridge-on-Wye. To the right of the bridge is the original ford used by drovers to drive their cattle through the river to markets in the Midlands and London.

The Wye Valley Walk

STAGE 4
Newbridge to Builth Wells

Start	Opposite Pen-y-Bont Farm, Newbridge-on-Wye SO 012 582
Finish	The Groe (beside the bull sculpture), Builth Wells SO 041 511
Distance	10.8km (6¾ miles)
Time	2hr 45min
Ascent	130m (425ft)
Terrain	750m stretch on verge of B4358; some farmland and woodland; mostly riverside walking
OS map	Explorer 200 Llandrindod Wells & Elan Valley
Refreshments	None on route (pub and shop in Newbridge)
Public toilets	None on route
Public transport	Bus service X47 between Rhayader and Llandrindod Wells stops at Newbridge (not Sundays). Railway station at Builth Road, just over 3km (1¾ miles) from Builth Wells and Cilmeri, 3.5km off the route to the west, on the same side of the river as the Wye Valley Walk. Note, there is no pedestrian bridge across the river between Builth Road Station and the Wye Valley Walk on the opposite bank

This is an easy stage with mostly gentle gradients, some field and woodland walking and a gorgeous 6km stretch beside the Wye. It starts with a 750m stretch of verge walking alongside the B4358. The first hour's walking is over fields and woodland, before joining up with the Wye at Cwrt-y-wernen Covert. The rest of the walk into Builth Wells is beside the Wye. A welcome picnic bench at Goetre Wood is well placed for a tea/coffee stop. A little further along pass three intriguing wooden sculptures beside the path, then Penddôl Rocks before arriving at the Groe in Builth Wells.

Newbridge to Goytre Wood (5km, 1hr 15min)
Standing opposite Pen-y-bont farm (at the junction of the B4358 with the Llysdinam road) turn right signposted for Beulah, to walk for 750m along the verge beside the

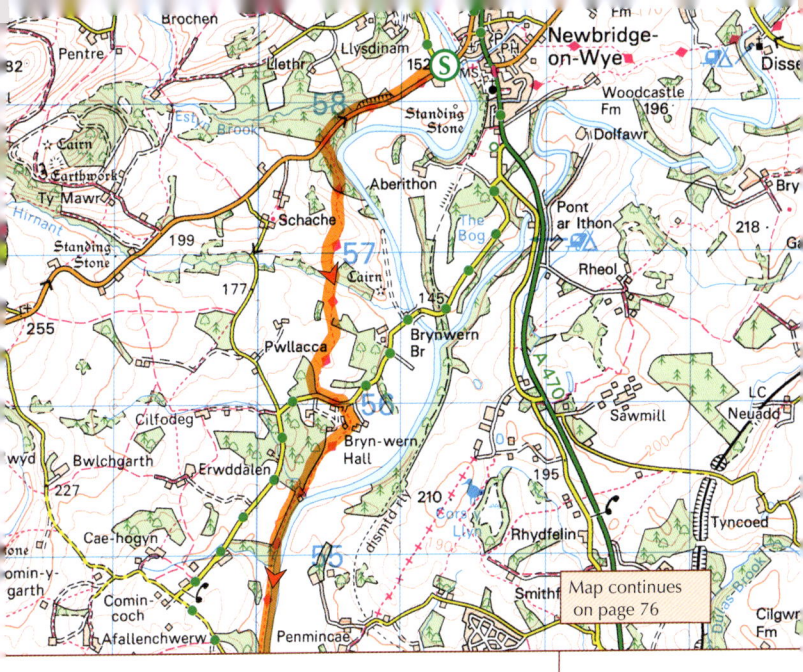

B4358. ▶ When the road levels out after the steep climb look out for a Wye Valley Walk signpost on the left and go through the gate. Follow the path down through Estyn Wood over four boardwalks and then through a gate into the field. Head diagonally uphill towards a gate in the fence, which comes into view as you climb. Go through the gate and follow the fence on your right, until a waymark directs you left, diagonally, to a signpost in the far left-hand corner of the field. Go down the zigzag path to cross the footbridge over the **Hirnant brook** and up the other side. Head straight across the field, through a gate and through the next field to another gate, where you turn left diagonally across the field to a waymarker on the edge of the copse. Go over the stile and follow the hedge on your right, through a gate. Follow the hedge to your left down to a pedestrian gate beside the wood.

Go through the gate and walk along the edge of the woodland to a kissing gate and out onto a minor road. (To access Cwm Wye Camping, leave the route here, turning

On the hilltop to your right looking out over the valley Llysdinam can be seen.

THE WYE VALLEY WALK

right, and follow the lane for 1.5km towards Pentrebach.) Turn left to walk along the road. Straight after the post box and Trederwen entrance turn right at a gateway into the wood. Follow the woodland path through a gate and then cross the field to a signpost and gate into the farmyard at Porthllwdd. Turn right to walk to the right of the farmyard, around the barn and through a gate into a field. Head diagonally rightish to follow the fence to the woodland. Go through the gate continuing alongside the field boundary until nearly at the end of the field, where several veteran oaks stand beside a stream. You are looking for a footbridge on the right, just after the last oak, which crosses the stream into the woodland. (It may be difficult to spot at first in the undergrowth.) Cross the bridge and go through the gate following the path uphill past an old building. **The River Wye** is now on your left and the path runs through lovely woods above the river. Cross another footbridge and go through the gate into the field to walk beside the Wye. Continue beside the river and after a while you reach a beautifully situated picnic bench on a bend in the river at Goytre Wood.

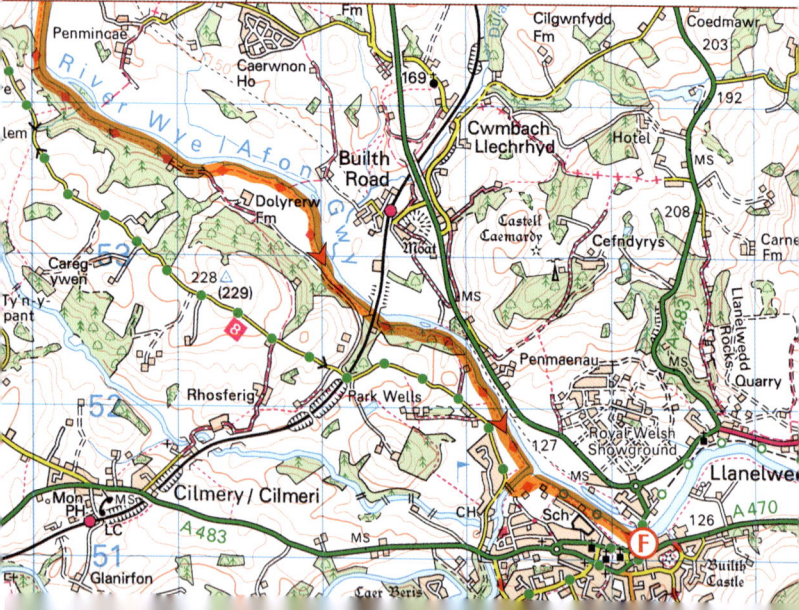

Taking in the view near Goytre Wood (photo: Emma Drabble)

Goytre Wood to Builth Wells (5.8km, 1hr 30min)

Soon after, where the track climbs uphill, keep left staying close to the river on a narrow path, which widens and runs through gorgeous woodland with the sound of the river rushing over rapids. Continue beside the Wye and pass three wooden sculptures to your right. Soon after, join a minor road continuing beside the river and cross a cattle grid. (To access Pwllgwilym accommodation, pub and railway station in Cilmeri, leave the route here before Plum Tree Pool, following the bridleway and footpath for 3.5km.) Turn left immediately through a gate into the field. Keep left to walk through a series of lovely riverside fields and then under the railway bridge, which carries trains on the Heart of Wales line.

Stay on the path through more fields and gates, passing Penddôl Rocks. When you can see the road bridge at **Builth Wells**, and houses to your right, bear right at the end of the field along the fence and then go to the left up to a gate in the corner of the field. Go through the gate, bear left and then turn left over the bridge. At the bottom of the steps turn left passing the skate park and walking along an avenue of trees in the Groe, Builth Wells' riverside park.

THE WYE VALLEY WALK

Wooden sculptures beside the path nearing Builth Wells (photo: Emma Drabble)

In the 19th century it became fashionable to visit places with **mineral springs** to 'take the waters'. Builth had both saline water (at Park Wells) and sulphur springs (at Glanne Wells), making it a popular destination with visitors looking for health cures (even though the sulphur water was said to smell like gunpowder). Before long 'Wells' was added to 'Builth' to help promote the health benefits the town offered. This riverside area was traditionally used by townsfolk to graze and water their livestock, but with the arrival of the railway in the 1860s tourism boomed and it was turned into a pleasant public area with a boating pavilion and bandstand.

If you are collecting passport stamps look out for Bronwye B&B. It's on the right of the park, the last house next to the red brick wall, with the stamp on a small wooden wall box facing the park. This stage ends beside the life-sized bronze sculpture of a Welsh Black bull, by artist Gavin Fifield, at the very end of the park.

Stage 4 – Newbridge to Builth Wells

BUILTH WELLS

Builth (Buallt in Welsh) is thought to mean 'the wild ox of the wooded slope', referring to the ancient cattle that roamed this area. The town is full of connections to bulls, even the local rugby team are called 'the Bulls'. You can still see a bull (or two) at the Royal Welsh Show which takes place here every July. Europe's largest agricultural show is a lively mix of livestock, sheepdog trials, shearing, horticulture, honey, crafts, displays and music.

Builth Wells is a small but busy town, with places to stay and a number of independent shops including an antique shop housed inside the former Baptist chapel and a gourmet grocery store with a great range of Welsh products, where you can pick up a picnic for the walk. Check out what's on at the Wyeside Arts Centre, housed in the old market hall, which is now a lively entertainment space with a cinema, theatre and gallery. If your walk coincides with the Royal Welsh Show it will be difficult to find accommodation in the area and you may have to travel further afield to find a place to stay. Builth Road railway station, 3km north on the Heart of Wales Line, serves the town – although Cilmeri Station, 3km west of Builth Wells, may be more useful as it is on the same side of the river as the Wye Valley Walk.

STAGE 5
Builth Wells to Erwood

Start	The Groe, Builth Wells (beside the bull sculpture) SO 041 511
Finish	Erwood Station Craft Centre SO 088 439
Distance	11.9km (7½ miles)
Time	3hr 50min
Ascent	465m (1525ft)
Terrain	Open common land and hillsides, some farmland; steep in places; some road walking on quiet lanes
OS map	Explorer 188 Builth Wells
Refreshments	None on route; at Builth Wells and Erwood Station Craft Centre
Public toilets	None on route; at Builth Wells and Erwood Station Craft Centre during opening hours
Public transport	Bus service T4 Builth Wells to Brecon runs between Builth Wells and Erwood (except Sundays and public holidays) and stops on request at Erwood Bridge; bus service X15 Builth to Hereford runs between Builth Wells and Erwood, stops on request at Erwood Bridge (Wednesdays only); Builth Road railway station 3km (1.8 miles) from Builth Wells (but on the opposite side of the river to the Wye Valley Walk) on the Heart of Wales Line between Shrewsbury and Swansea

There are quite a few steep ups and downs on this stage, but the rewards are some of the best views on the Walk, looking back into Mid Wales, south to the Black Mountains (with a tantalising glimpse of the Bannau Brycheiniog (Brecon Beacons) and east to Aberedw Hill. Leaving Builth Wells you pass the grassy ruins of Builth Castle before climbing for about a mile along a country lane. A short downhill takes you to the River Duhonw, followed by another climb along an enclosed gravel track. Footpaths and farm tracks continue the climb up to the open moorland of Banc y Celyn, where the wide skies and expansive views continue for about 3km and the path is mostly level. It's virtually all downhill then along a minor road across Little Hill Common, with a wonderful photo opportunity looking out over the Wye towards Erwood Bridge. There is one final uphill section across fields and common land before descending from Twmpath down a minor road to cross the A470 and the Wye, to arrive at Erwood Station Craft Centre.

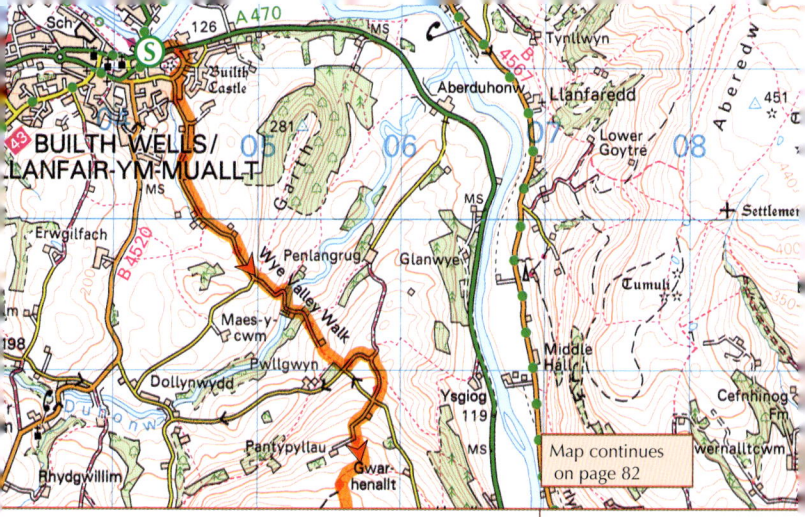

Builth Wells to highest point crossing Banc y Celyn (5.3km, 2hr)

From the bull sculpture in the Groe park walk towards the Wye Bridge and turn right in front of the Wyeside Centre, passing an amazing mural on the building to your right.

> The mural remembers **Llewelyn ap Gruffydd**, the last true Prince of Wales before the title was re-used by Edward I and given to the male heir to the English throne. Llewelyn died just outside Builth Wells in 1282, trying to drive the English out of Welsh territory. His death marked the end of organised resistance to English rule in Wales and claims to Welsh independence effectively died with him. His head was sent to the English King, Edward I, who just five years before had built a substantial stone fortress in Builth.

Turn left in front of the Lion Inn to walk along Castle Street. Take the first right to continue along Castle Street, and bear right skirting around the site of **Builth Castle** on your right. If you wish to explore the castle, a stile on the right leads into a field, where sheep graze among the thistles and nettles on top of the castle mound.

THE WYE VALLEY WALK

Builth Castle was originally built as a wooden motte-and-bailey castle by Phillip de Braose shortly after the Norman invasion of England in 1066, to control a strategic river crossing. The grass-covered remains of the castle date from 1277, when it was rebuilt by Edward I to strengthen English defences.

Turn left along Newry Road. Cross Tanhouse Bridge. Stay on this road for just under 1.5km, passing Sunny Bank. At the junction keep left along the dead-end road. You will soon hear the river below as you follow the road steeply downhill. Cross the **Duhonw** via the footbridge. Walk to the left of a house going uphill along the gravel lane enclosed by hedges and trees. At the road turn left along a restricted byway, with lovely views to the north, which widens out further along. At the road go straight across, along a track signed Pantypyllau. As you climb the view opens up to the right towards Builth Wells and the Royal Welsh Showground.

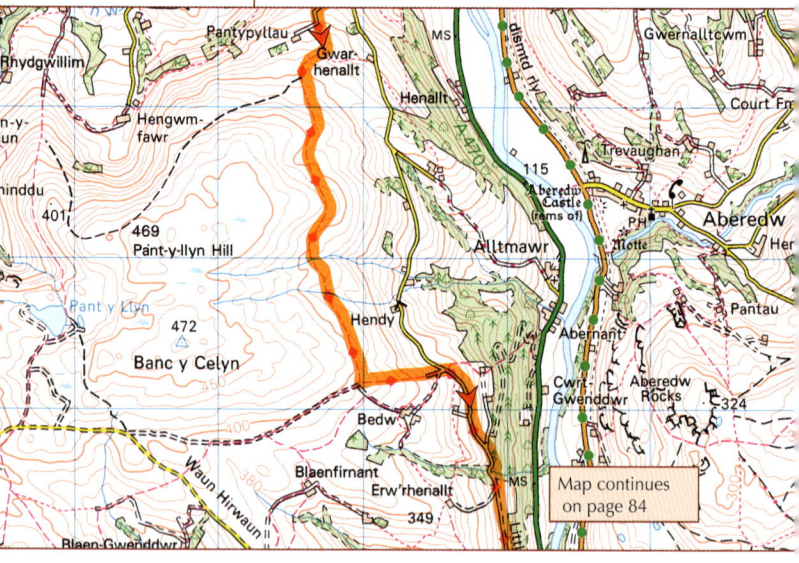

Map continues on page 84

Stage 5 – Builth Wells to Erwood

Looking towards Builth Wells

When the gravel track bears right to **Pantypyllau** (B&B accommodation here), keep left up a grassy path to a gate. Go through the gate and keep to the path on the left-hand field edge, following it round and uphill. Go through another gate and follow the fence on the left up to open moorland and a waymarker where you turn left and continue alongside the fence. Soon the Black Mountains and Bannau Brycheiniog come into view. Go through another gate and continue beside the fence, passing a section of very old slate wall and a small conifer plantation. Pass through two gates in quick succession, the highest point on this stage.

Banc y Celyn to Erwood Station Craft Centre (6.6km, 1hr 50min)

Then head across field (with a pond below) along an old hedge line to go through a gate. Follow the track (through bracken in summer) turning left immediately onto a more defined track heading to the right of the

THE WYE VALLEY WALK

> To get your first view of Pen y Fan, the highest mountain in South Wales, walk a few feet past the left turn.

mountains in the distance. Go over two small streams. Ignore the track to the left when you reach a crossroads of tracks. Keep straight on until you come to a junction at a fence. ◀ Turn left at the junction and walk downhill beside the fence on the right, with far-reaching views to your left to the village of Aberedw and Llewelyn's Cave on the opposite side of the river.

PRINCE LLEWELYN AP GRUFFYDD

Llewelyn ap Gruffydd, the Prince of Gwynedd, was the only Welsh ruler to be recognised as Prince of Wales by the English. In 1282 he was at war with the English King Edward I, but after defeat, legend has it he hid in a cave at Aberedw Rocks. He asked a local blacksmith to reverse the horseshoes on his horse so it would look if he was travelling in the opposite direction. Betrayed by the blacksmith, Llewelyn was killed near Irfon Bridge, decapitated, and his head displayed in the Tower of London. It is said that the monks of the Abbey of Cwmhir claimed his body.

Follow the path down to a gate and keep straight on down to the road where you turn right, to walk along the road for about 2km. After a while **Little Hill Common** opens out to the left, with gorgeous views down to river, Erwood Bridge and the Black Mountains beyond. The road starts to descend, zigzagging down and passing New House on the right. After New House, when the road

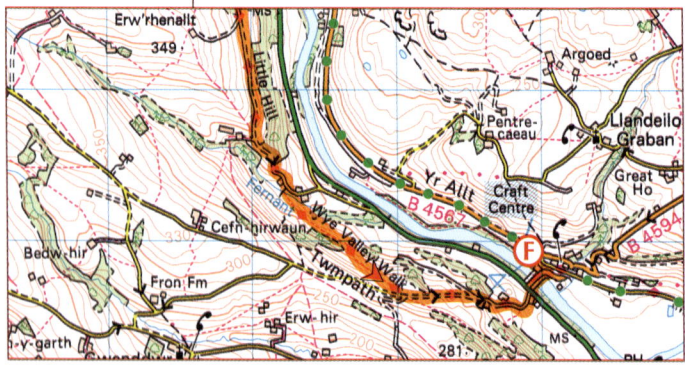

STAGE 5 – BUILTH WELLS TO ERWOOD

COMMON LAND

Crossing common land on Banc y Celyn

This stage of the walk passes through areas of common land on Banc y Celyn, Little Hill and Twmpath, and enjoys fabulous views over vast expanses of common land to the east of the Wye on Aberedw and Llandeilo Hill. About 8.4 per cent of Wales is registered as common land, where 'commoners' historically have certain rights to graze sheep or cattle (pasturage), take peat or turf for fuel (turbary), take wood or gorse (estovers), fish (piscary) and graze pigs on acorns and beech-mast (pannage). Common land has been crucially important to many farms in Wales and without these grazing rights they would not be viable.

Generally, common land has not been improved for agricultural purposes, making it of great value for wildlife, especially species of farmland birds which are in decline. Of particular importance to wildlife is the mixture of vegetation – grass, heathland, bracken, scrub, hawthorn and gorse – which develops between the lower, enclosed and more intensively managed fields and the higher unenclosed hill and moorland. In Welsh this habitat is called *Ffridd* and it provides vital habitat for upland birds such as whinchat, yellowhammer, linnet, wheatear and redstart.

curves left, look out for a path on the right dropping down to a footbridge. Cross the **Fernant** stream (SO 072 443) and turn left at the end of the bridge. Just after going through a gate the track forks. Take the right-hand fork, ignoring the track joining on the right. After a scrubby section the

THE WYE VALLEY WALK

path soon opens out and starts climbing for a short distance. Very soon you meet a junction of tracks, with a large ash tree just to the left. Take the left-hand fork (which may be difficult to see when the bracken is at full height) to enter an old lane running between the hedges and trees. If the lane is overgrown duck left to walk through the field beside the hedge. Reaching the fence, walk to the right of it and continue along the fence to your left. Go through the gate and uphill onto Twmpath common. Head straight on uphill (on a path through bracken during the summer months), going slightly to the right and crossing a couple of wet areas, before reaching the road.

(To reach Erwood village for B&B accommodation and pub, leave the route here, cross the road and continue on the footpath to Maescletwr and then down into Erwood.

Looking towards Erwood and the Black Mountains from Little Hill Common

STAGE 5 – BUILTH WELLS TO ERWOOD

This avoids walking along the busy A470, which has no footway between Erwood bridge and Erwood village.)

Turn left to walk downhill, over a cattle grid, and down to the A470. Buses between Builth Wells, Brecon and Hay-on-Wye can be hailed here. (To reach Pwll-y-faedda B&B, leave the route at the A470 and turn left to walk along the wide grass verge. The B&B is 0.4km further on the right.)

Turn left and cross the road to walk over Erwood Bridge. (To access accommodation on this side of the river, leave the route at the end of the bridge and continue on the road. Turn right onto the B4594. After 0.3km turn right for the B&B at The Skreen, or after 1.8km turn left for Great House Farm glamping.) Turn left at the end of the bridge and go through a gate to the right of the house, following a narrow path up to the carpark at **Erwood Station Craft Centre** where this stage ends.

> From 1864 the Mid Wales Railway ran between Llanidloes and Brecon, with a station at Erwood. When the railway was axed in 1962 the station closed, but in 1984 Alan Cunningham, a professional wood turner, gave the railway station a new life when he restored the site to exhibit his work. Two 19th-century carriages from Rhosgoch and Eardisley, and a signal box from Newbridge-on-Wye, were acquired to make extra gallery space and they are still in use today at what is now **Erwood Station Craft Centre**. It's a great place to refuel at the end of your walk between Builth Wells and Erwood.

ERWOOD

Erwood village is about 1km south of Erwood Bridge. As there is no footway it is not recommended to walk to the village along the very busy A470, the main north/south route through Wales. There is a pub, accommodation and public toilets in the village and a regular bus service (T4 between Builth Wells and Brecon) which can be hailed at Erwood Bridge to alight in Erwood village (and vice versa)

Very low water in the Wye at Erwood Bridge

STAGE 6
Erwood to Glasbury

Start	Erwood Station Craft Centre SO 088 439
Finish	Glasbury Bridge SO 178 392
Distance	14km (8¾ miles)
Time	3hr 15min
Ascent	70m (230ft)
Terrain	Mostly tracks and field paths; some road sections (including 200m stretch on A470 near Erwood)
OS map	Explorer 188 Builth Wells
Refreshments	Llangoed Hall Hotel, Boughrood Village Stores, Bridge End Inn, Llyswen (5min off route at Boughrood). Glasbury: Foyles restaurant, Paddler's Rest Café at the River Wye Activity Centre, Harp Inn, Glasbury Service Station
Public toilets	Erwood Station Craft Centre (when open), Glasbury north side, just before the Wye Bridge
Public transport	Bus service T14 between Brecon and Hereford runs through Glasbury. Bus service X15 Builth Wells to Hereford calls at Boughrood, Erwood and Glasbury (Wednesdays only). Bus service T4 Builth Wells to Brecon stops at Erwood (you can also hail it at Erwood Bridge start/end of section) (not Sundays and public holidays)

This stage begins with 3.5km of easy walking along a minor road to Llanstephan Bridge, and 200m on the verge beside the A470. A peaceful riverside section follows through fields from where you catch glimpses of the Black Mountains and pass Llangoed Hall Hotel. This stretch from just south of Llanstephan Bridge (opposite Trericket Mill) down to Boughrood is stile free. A short walk along a quiet lane is followed by pavement walking through Boughrood. The final few miles are through fields and along farm tracks with lovely views of the Black Mountains. A short section on a minor road brings you to Glasbury.

STAGE 6 – ERWOOD TO GLASBURY

Erwood Station Craft Centre to Boughrood (8.2km, 2hr 5min)

From Erwood Station turn right and walk along the road to the junction with a minor road on the right. Turn right, signposted Boughrood. Cross the cattle grid and bridge and stay on this road, ignoring turnings off to the left or right.

After 3.5km take the first turning on the right, just before the sign for Llanstephan, which leads down to an elegant and very narrow bridge. ▶

Llanstephan Bridge is the only wooden-decked vehicular suspension bridge in Wales. You can hear the distinctive rumble as traffic crosses the wooden planks long before you reach the bridge. There is a 4mph speed limit on the bridge for obvious reasons. It was built in 1922 by David Rowell and Co of Westminster, who also constructed Foy Bridge which you pass on Stage 12.

Llanstephan Bridge (photo: Emma Drabble)

This was the route of the former Mid Wales Railway along which trains ran from Brecon to Llanidloes from 1865 to 1962.

THE WYE VALLEY WALK

Cross the bridge and turn left to walk beside the A470 on the grass verge for a very short distance. At the end of the metal road barrier, opposite **Trericket Mill** (SO 113 414), turn left through a kissing gate into the field.

STAGE 6 – ERWOOD TO GLASBURY

Walk along the left-hand fence boundary and through a gate into woodland. Go through another gate into a field. The path continues through fields for about 2.5km, keeping close to the river and passing through a series of pedestrian gates and gateways. Rounding a corner, the Black Mountains will suddenly come into view in the distance, while to the right you pass **Llangoed Hall Hotel**, with its red brick, walled garden and tall brick chimneys.

Llangoed Hall is probably best known as 'the Laura Ashley hotel', having been saved from demolition in the 1980s by Welsh fashion designer Laura Ashley's husband Sir Bernard Ashley, who turned the neglected mansion into a luxury hotel. It was constructed in the 1630s in classic Jacobean style and has had many owners, including one who lost the house in a card game! In the 20th century it was remodeled by Sir Bertram Clough Williams-Ellis (of Portmeirion fame) in his first major architectural commission. If you fancy a bit of luxury splash out on afternoon tea or an overnight stay!

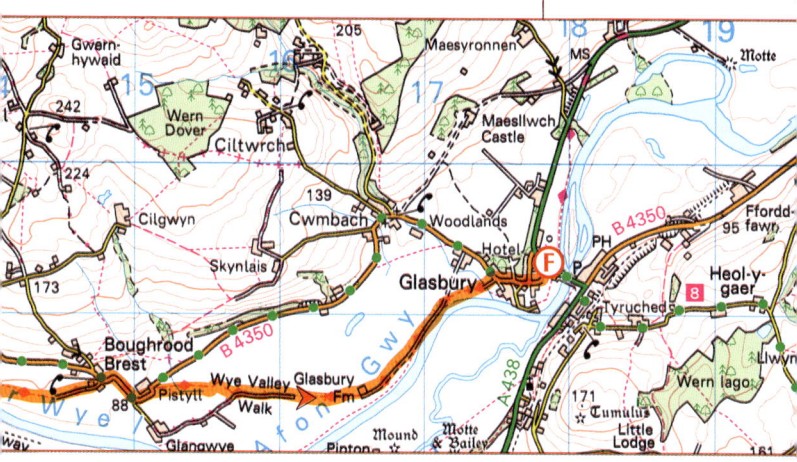

Magnificent sweet chestnut trees close to Llangoed Hall

Continue along the path and eventually go through a gate onto a tarmac lane at the water treatment works. Stay on this lane until it reaches the B4350 at **Boughrood** (SO 129 384). (To access pubs, shop and accommodation 0.5km away in Llyswen, leave the route here, turning right, and then turn left at the A470.)

Boughrood to Glasbury (5.8km, 1hr 10min)
Turn left on the road to cross the bridge into Boughrood.

Boughrood, or Bochrwyd/Bachrwyd in Welsh, probably takes its name from the amazing bend the river makes here, looping right back on itself. (In Welsh 'river bend' is *bach* and 'ford' is *rhyd*). Crossing the bridge you pass the old toll house on your right, which until 1934 levied tolls from travellers to pay for the construction of the bridge. There is a unique building in the churchyard of nearby St Cynog's Church, the only parish mortuary to survive in Wales. It dates from the 1850s, around the time that the church was rebuilt.

STAGE 6 – ERWOOD TO GLASBURY

Walk through Boughrood village, passing a small shop on the right, and continue on past the speed limit signs for a short distance until reaching the Old Rectory, the last house on the right. Turn right down the driveway and follow the right of way through the Old Rectory garden and grounds, walking around the house to the right, straight across the lawn beside the house, and through the gate onto a woodland path. Stay on this path above the river, ignoring tracks on the right down to the waterside.

Go through the gate into the field and follow the hedge to your left. Lovely views to the Black Mountains soon appear in front. Go through another gate and follow the hedge on the left, keeping to the hedge as the track becomes fenced in on the right. Go through two more gates. At the B4350 turn right signposted for Glasbury along a short stretch to **Pistyll**. Leave the road in front of Pistyll farmhouse through a pedestrian gate on the right, onto a hedge-lined track which opens up into a field. Follow the hedge on the left and go through another gate. Continue alongside the hedge and into another field, curving round to the right to walk in front of a stone ruin, Pwll-y-baw (Welsh for 'mucky pool'), and enter a tree-lined path. At the gate turn left onto a track (SO 156 384). You may have to open and close a number of gates as you follow this track all the way to Glasbury.

Pass a huge oak tree and go through another gate. The valley of the River Wye has opened out, with a wide flood plain and arable fields, in contrast to the steep grassland meadows further north. Go through another gate, keeping beside the hedge. Walk through the field and keep straight on ignoring gates to either side, through more gateways, and passing **Glasbury Farm** on the left. Stay on the track through more gates, eventually passing a riverside fishermen's hut. Go through the gate here and stay on the fenced track, ignoring gates to left and right, to reach the B4350 (SO 175 392). Turn right and walk into **Glasbury**, passing Foyles hotel and restaurant on the left. Look out for the River Wye Activity Centre on the right, where you can collect your passport stamp at the Paddler's Rest Café.

THE WYE VALLEY WALK

> The Scout Hut was opened by Robert Baden-Powell, founder of the scouting movement in the 1920s, making this (possibly) the oldest purpose-built scout hut in Wales still in use.

This stage ends at Glasbury Bridge, so after collecting your stamp continue on the B4350 for a short distance. Bear slightly right to walk through the car park, passing toilets and the Scout Hut. ◄ Take the ramp up to the A438. Cross the road and walk along the pavement to enjoy the views from Glasbury Bridge. Note the steps down to the left just before the bridge, which is the start of Stage 7 Glasbury to Hay-on-Wye.

GLASBURY

The Wye splits the village of Glasbury in two. There are public toilets on the east side, before Glasbury Bridge. Also on this side of the river are Foyles restaurant and hotel and the River Wye Activity Centre and Paddler's Rest Café. On the west bank there is a service station and pub with rooms (Harp Inn). Glasbury has become a popular canoe destination with several operators hiring canoes. There are a number of accommodation options in Glasbury and the surrounding countryside.

Fisherman's hut at Glasbury

STAGE 7

Glasbury to Hay-on-Wye

Start	Glasbury Bridge, (north downstream side) SO 178 392
Finish	Wye Bridge, Hay-on-Wye, SO 228 425
Distance	8.2km (5 miles)
Time	2hr 50min
Ascent	165m (540ft)
Terrain	Riverside fields; 0.8 km on verge beside A438; uphill section on lane; wooded path; field descent to Llowes; steep climb after Llowes followed by steep descent to A438, then riverbank path
OS map	Explorer OL13 Brecon Beacons National Park or Explorer 201 Knighton & Presteigne and Explorer 188 Builth Wells
Refreshments	Harp Inn in Glasbury and service station shop both on south side of Glasbury Bridge (more options on the north side of the bridge, along previous section)
Public toilets	Glasbury Bridge (north side), Hay-on-Wye by clock tower and beside Craft Centre next to the main car park in Oxford Road
Public transport	Hereford to Brecon bus service T14 stops at Glasbury, Clyro and Hay-on-Wye. The nearest railway station is Hereford

Easy river valley walking following mainly field-edge paths with an 800m section on the verge beside the A438, and a short section of quiet lane. There is a stone cross to view at St Meilig's Church in Llowes, while a steep climb and descent after Llowes rewards with stunning views of the Black Mountains and Bannau Brycheiniog (Brecon Beacons). A gentle walk beside the river brings you to Hay-on-Wye.

Note: In the past the Wye Valley Walk continued along the A438 from Llowes towards Clyro for 1km, before following the riverside footpath to Hay-on-Wye. Today the A438 is a busy road with heavy, fast-moving vehicles, making for a less than pleasing walking experience. The off-road route from Llowes via Briwnant is recommended, especially because of the stunning views. Your OS map may still show the old roadside route.

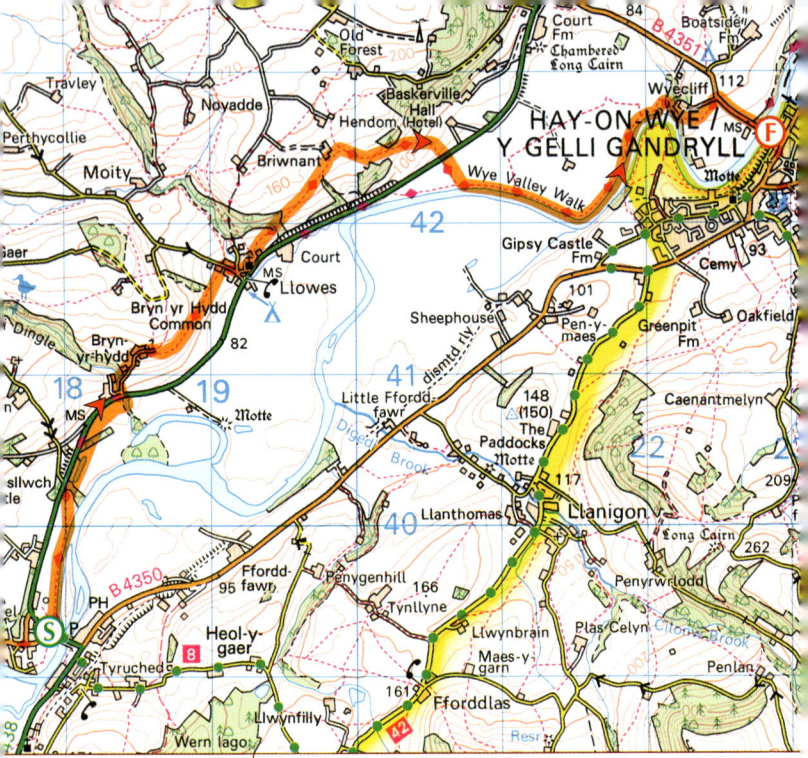

Glasbury to Llowes (3.2km, 1hr)

At Glasbury Bridge (north side), take the steps down to the left immediately before the river. Walk through the field beside an avenue of poplar trees full of mistletoe. Pass the water treatment works and go through a gate, turning right to walk along the field edge passing through a series of gates until you reach a concrete water trough on your left. Now head diagonally left across the field to a gate in the far corner of the field. Go through the gate, cross the old road, through another gate and then up to the A438 (SO 179 401). Turn right to walk on the grass verge for 800m. After the uphill section levels out, turn left after Little Mill Cottages to walk up a lane. Keep climbing and where the tarmac stops continue on the gravel track walking between buildings at **Bryn-yr-rhydd**

STAGE 7 – GLASBURY TO HAY-ON-WYE

Farm. After the last barn on the right, turn right immediately along a walled path with views towards the Black Mountains. At the end of this short, walled section turn right. The path goes through scrubby woodland with some veteran trees eventually emerging through a gate into a field looking towards the hamlet of Llowes, with lovely views of Hay Bluff and Lord Hereford's Knob or Twmpa. Walk downhill to the right of the fence heading for the houses. Go through a gate in the left corner of the field, then over a stile and through a kissing gate to come out on the road. Turn right and walk down past the houses into **Llowes**, turning left over a bridge and into the churchyard of St Meilig's Church.

ST MEILIG'S CHURCH, LLOWES

St Meilig brought Christianity to Llowes when he established a small monastery here in the 6th century. The name 'Llowes' may have come from St Llywes, another monk who settled in the area at that time. By the late 12th century, a hermit called Wechelen lived in a cell attached to the church, which had an opening through which he could watch the priest at the alter and receive food and drink. In the 19th century the medieval church was in a dangerous state of repair and was rebuilt. The lower part of the tower is all that survives from the medieval period.

Inside the church is a monumental sandstone slab with ancient cross carvings and the remains of a scratch dial. This was a type of sun dial used from the 12th century onwards to show the time of services, rather than the time of day. In the past this stone was called the Moll Walbee stone. Mol was a giantess who built Hay Castle in one night, gathering boulders from Glasbury and carrying them in her apron to Hay. After one annoying rock fell on her foot, she hurled it across the Wye where it landed in Llowes churchyard. Mol Walbee was a real person, Maude de Haia (Hay), wife of William de Breos, Lord of Brecknock and you can find out more about her life by visiting Hay Castle at the end of this stage. In 1952 the cross was scheduled as an ancient monument and moved into the church for protection in 1956. Diarist Francis Kilvert was a friend of the rector of St Meilig's, Rev Thomas Williams, and often visited the church. In the churchyard you can find a sundial dedicated to Kilvert which was erected by the Kilvert Society.

THE WYE VALLEY WALK

Llowes to Hay-on-Wye (5km, 1hr 50min)

Walk past the church and leave the churchyard through the kissing gate. (To access Seren Bach Campsite, leave the route here, turning right to walk along the A438 for a couple of minutes. The campsite is on the left.) Cross the lane to take a track up to a gate into the field. Follow the track uphill to the right, leading to the woods. Stop to catch your breath and look back at the gorgeous views behind you. Go through the gateway into woodland and stay on the track climbing to a stile into another field. Cross the stile and follow the hedge on the left. From the top of this field look back again to see the Bannau Brycheiniog behind you. Go through the gate and follow the hedge on the left past **Briwnant** to a gate, with a communication mast visible in the distance. Go through the gate and head straight across the field. Turn right before the gate and follow the hedge downhill to woodland, to go through another gate. Walk diagonally downhill towards the A438, crossing a wet gully. Skirt around the forestry on the left and head very steeply diagonally downhill, heading to the roadside fence beyond the concrete area.

Ahead to your left is the **Baskerville Hall Hotel**, the former home of the Baskerville family who were

Hay Bluff and Lord Hereford's Knob (Twmpa) from Briwnant

friends of Sir Arthur Conan Doyle. It's said he had the idea for the Sherlock Holmes book *The Hound of the Baskervilles* while staying at the hall.

Beyond Baskerville Hall is the village of Clyro, where the **Reverend Robert Francis Kilvert** was curate from 1865 to 1872. He was one of the finest nature and travel writers of the 19th century. Today this area between Clyro and Bredwardine is known as Kilvert Country.

Go through the pedestrian gate, cross the A438 and through another gate to walk along a track which soon meets the riverside path. Turn left to continue beside the river for about 1.8km, eventually passing a house opposite The Warren. Soon afterwards look for a footbridge on the right which leads into the wood, following a path uphill past a tall retaining wall for **Wyecliff** on the left. Go through the gate to a surprise view of Hay Castle and the town. Keep left through the field (sometimes a camping field), following the hedge on your left up to the B4351. Turn right and cross the road to walk on the pavement (also the route of Offa's Dyke Path National Trail) to Hay Bridge, the end of this stage.

The Wye Valley Walk

HAY-ON-WYE

Richard Booth, who opened Hay-on-Wye's first book shop in 1961, single-handedly put Hay-on-Wye on the map as the bookshop capital of the world. On 1 April 1977, the border town of Hay-on-Wye was proclaimed an independent kingdom, when the slightly eccentric Booth declared himself the King of Hay and took the liberty of issuing passports to locals! Hay Castle, now a centre for arts, literature and learning, is entitled to bestow peerages in the tradition of the King of Hay. The titles are not real in any legal sense – you can't use them on your passport or driving licence, but you can use them casually whenever you want, with your name entered in the Hay Peerage archive.

Hay-on-Wye

STAGE 7 – GLASBURY TO HAY-ON-WYE

Hay Castle

Hay is a lively, historic market town, straddling the border between Wales and England. As well as finding bookshops on every corner, there are also many independent shops, galleries and potteries to discover. There are plenty of places to eat, drink and stay (although finding accommodation in the area during the Hay Festival is almost impossible). Hay's annual literary festival is held at the end of May/early June and attracts novelists, Nobel prize winners, politicians, historians, musicians, environmentalists and scientists from around the world. For evening entertainment check out what's on at the Globe at Hay, an independent arts centre hosting live music, plays and exhibitions. It is also home to the Institute of Art and Ideas, a charity founded to promote free thinking, creativity and debate. The Tourist Information Bureau is opposite the main car park in Oxford Road where buses stop. Collect your passport stamp at FW Golesworthy & Sons, purveyors of outdoor clothing and equipment on Broad Street.

STAGE 8

Hay-on-Wye to Bredwardine

Start	Wye Bridge, Hay-on-Wye, SO 228 425
Finish	Red Lion Hotel, Bredwardine, SO 331 444
Distance	14km (8½ miles)
Time	4hr 45min
Ascent	440m (1445ft)
Terrain	Undulating route; very steep climb up Merbach Hill; descent into Bredwardine
OS map	Explorer 201 Knighton & Presteigne
Refreshments	There are no refreshment stops on this section (or on the following two sections into Hereford), so make sure to stock up before leaving Hay-on-Wye; Red Lion Hotel in Bredwardine
Public toilets	None on route
Public transport	Bus service 447 between Bredwardine and Hereford (one early and one late bus Monday to Friday); Bus service 448 between Bredwardine and Hereford (one bus each way Tuesdays and Thursdays); bus service T14 Brecon to Hereford passes through Hay-on-Wye (not Sundays)

Leaving Wales behind as you cross the Dulas Brook, marking the Wales-England boundary, this stage passes through border country. This was the land of the Norman Marcher lords and the route passes a motte-and-bailey at Lower Castleton. The stage ends with a steep climb up to Merbach Hill, which at 305m gives expansive views towards the Welsh mountains, across the Herefordshire Plain and to the Malverns. The bridleway here may have been an old drovers' route bringing livestock to the markets of the Midlands and London. There is a steep descent down to the small village of Bredwardine

Hay-on-Wye to Priory Farm (4km, 1hr 10min)

From the Wye Bridge walk towards the town and turn left down Broad Street. Straight after the Globe at Hay on the right, look out for stone steps beside a blue plaque marking the site of the town well. Turn right up the steps, through a gate, signposted Black Lion Inn. Go through

STAGE 8 – HAY-ON-WYE TO BREDWARDINE

another gate onto a narrow road. Walk between a few houses and after No 4, on the left, turn sharp left back on yourself downhill. Walk across the small parking area. Turn left over the footbridge. After nearly 100km of walking through Wales you cross the Dulas Brook and into England. Go through a gate and follow the track to the left in front of the house.

Head diagonally right across the field towards a gate which will become visible shortly. Go through the gate and down to the left to cross a stream and through a pedestrian gate on the left. Turn right to a gate in the right-hand corner of the field. Go through the pedestrian gate and turn right along the lane. Very soon the lane bears right but keep straight on past the house on the left, through a gate into a field, to follow the hedge on your right. Go through another gate, keeping beside the hedge and through a third gate at an oak tree. Cut across the field to reach the hedge corner directly in front of you. At the corner continue beside the hedge on your left, heading for a gate. Go through the gate and continue on the same line straight across the field to an avenue of trees. Pass through the gate and cross the tree-lined track, to continue on the same line over the next field. Go through the gateway following the fence to your right.

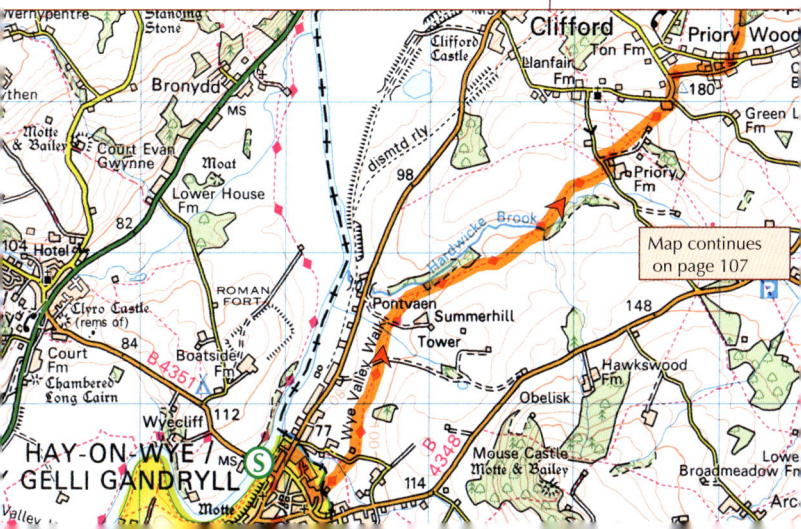

Cross the stile at the brook and another stile into the orchard. Head straight across to the waymarker in the middle of the orchard. Cross the tarmac access lane and head for the next marker and gate. Go through the kissing gate and continue, keeping to the hedge on the right. When the fence on your right ends keep straight on heading for the trees, which the path winds through. Where it starts to climb gently, the path goes left of the trees heading for a waymarker. After the waymarker keep on the same line, passing a bench on left. The path gently curves to the right towards another waymarker and a stile beyond. Go over the stile and walk diagonally right towards the hedge on your right and follow it down to cross the **Hardwicke Brook**.

Continue uphill through the gateway and walk beside the hedge to your left to a gate in the distance. Go through the gate and follow a rutted track uphill as it bears round to the right and another gate. Stay on the track up to **Priory Farm**, go over the stile and turn left along the road.

> An eclipse of the moon was witnessed at **Priory Farm** by Francis Kilvert in 1870, when he visited the Allen family to observe this rare occurrence. The house dates back to the reign of Henry I when a local lord, Simon Fitz Richard, granted land to the Cluniac Order to establish a cell for monks, which later became a priory. At the dissolution of the monasteries by Henry VIII in 1536, the land and buildings were taken over by the Crown and sold off to loyal families. Priory Farm eventually became the property of Benjamin Haigh Allen, who was High Sheriff of Herefordshire in the mid-1800s. By this time the farmhouse was a substantial Georgian building, probably constructed with stone from the priory.

Priory Farm to Locksters Pool Farm (2.1km, 50min)
Very soon turn right over a cattle grid and stile for Priory Gardens. When you are level with the farm buildings leave the gravel track, going slight left and heading

northeast towards the houses and lone tree on the horizon. (To access bell tent camping, glamping and self-catering accommodation at Drover's Road, turn right when you are level with the first house on the right, passing to the left of the house and following footpaths for 4km to reach Llanerch-y-coed.)

Nearing the houses head to the left of the wooden-clad house, from where you will spot the next stile. ▶ Go over this stile and then straight across the field to a stile to the right of the houses. Cross this stile and go up a narrow path to the road. Cross the road and continue uphill signposted Clifford and Whitney. Very soon (opposite Pear Tree house) turn right before the road junction. Follow the short cut through the play and picnic area. At the road turn right. Continue until you reach Priory Hall on the right.

Turn left here, along a public footpath across a small area of community orchard. Cross the tarmac lane in front of the telegraph pole and take a narrow path immediately to the right of it. Go through the gate and follow the path beside the hedge on the left. Go through another gate and through the field beside the right-hand hedge, crossing a footbridge and a stile and continuing beside the hedge down to a gate onto the road. Turn right passing a bench on the left made from old railway track and continue until you reach a stone bridge.

(Leave the route here, crossing the bridge and following the Herefordshire Trail, to access camping at Locksters Pool Farm, on the right after 0.3km. Continue on the Herefordshire Trail and cross the Wye at Whitney Bridge for Whitney Bridge Glamping.

Make sure to look behind you to enjoy the view back to the Bannau Brycheiniog/Brecon Beacons.

Locksters Pool Farm to Merbach Hill (4.7km, 1hr 50min)
Immediately before the bridge, turn right through the gate and down to the old railway line. Turn right for a short distance along the embankment to a gate and stile.

> 'The Thunderer', as the **Golden Valley Railway** was known, was built as a narrow-gauge railway to improve trade and communications in what was then a fairly remote area, between Pontrilas and Hay-on-Wye. It was never a financial success. The line running to Hay-on-Wye opened in 1889 and, having run out of money, closed in 1898. It was bought for a knock-down price by the Great Western Railway, who reopened the route in 1901. The last train to Hay-on-Wye ran in 1949.

Go over the stile and continue on the farm track. Soon views to the Wye and the Herefordshire Plain open up in front.

> The Wye meanders across a wide floodplain here, making a loop at **Locksters Pool**, one of several famous salmon pools on this stretch of river. Wildfowl often gather in this area during the winter months, including wigeon, teal and goosander, and occasionally migratory Bewick's swans, with their musical trumpeting calls and yellow-and-black bills.

Follow the track downhill to go through a gate and across the next field as the path curves to the right. Go through another gate and head straight on to the oak trees. Walk to the left of a monster oak, through a gate into the wood. Leave the woodland through a gate and head straight across the field, through another gate into more woodland. The path climbs uphill and through a gate into a field. Walk diagonally left across the field, heading for a gate below the house. Go through the gate. (To access The Smithy B&B, leave the route here and turn right to walk uphill past Upper Castleton Farm. Follow the footpath for 1.3km to Pen-y-Park.)

STAGE 8 – HAY-ON-WYE TO BREDWARDINE

Turn left along the road. Opposite Lower Castleton Farm you may be able to make out the remains of a motte and bailey castle to your left (privately owned), which has given the houses in this area their name. Follow the road as it curves to the right around Old Castleton and at the entrance to the house turn left through a gate into the field.

Follow the hedge on the left across two fields. Merbach Hill, the hefty climb at the end of this section, now looms in front! Go through the gate and turn right to walk beside a wooden fence and then along a gravel driveway. Go through another gate and turn left along the B4352 at **Clock Mills** Bridge, passing an impressive gateway. After a short roadside section pass the turning to Middlewood on the right and straightaway take the next footpath on the right between two hedges. The track becomes wider and passes a barn on the right at Home Farm. Keep straight on and immediately turn left at the sign for Merbach where the track splits by a dead-end sign. Stay on the track following it round to the right. The climb up **Merbach Hill** begins gradually, then gets steeper. Ignore gates off to either side, eventually reaching a pedestrian gate that leads into forestry. ▶

Just before this gate look left for a view of the Wye flowing through the fields.

Eleven counties are visible from the top of Merbach Hill

THE WYE VALLEY WALK

Go through the gate and turn right. Very soon keep right at the information panel and junction of paths. Soon, where the track forks, bear left around an old stone structure on the left and continue uphill. The path gets steeper in the woodland and this section can be muddy. ◀ The woodland eventually opens out with a field to the right. Continue through this open section, which may be covered in bracken in summer. After another uphill section the path flattens out and you turn left at the junction by a Wye Valley Walk marker (SO 304 447), where the Herefordshire Trail continues to the right to the top of Merbach Hill.

An unofficial, narrow path runs parallel to the official route avoiding mud and overgrown vegetation.

It is worth taking a short detour along the Herefordshire Trail to the trig point on **Merbach Hill** with its panoramic views. The trig is to the left when you reach the summit.

Merbach Hill is 318m high, from where it is claimed you can see 11 counties on a clear day. The area around the summit has many dips and bumps where quarrying has taken place. Merbach Common was once an important grazing area for local farms and the Wye Valley Walk follows a bridleway that was probably an old drovers' route taking cattle and livestock to the markets of the Midlands and London.

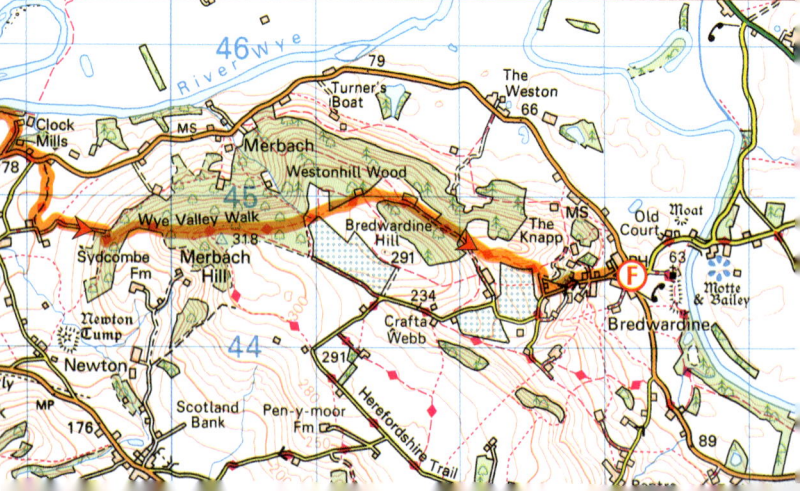

STAGE 8 – HAY-ON-WYE TO BREDWARDINE

Merbach Hill to Bredwardine (3.2km, 55min)

Continue along the Wye Valley Walk following waymarkers. Turn left at the crossroads of paths. When you reach another junction of paths, beside an information panel, go straight ahead through the pedestrian gate. Cross two fields and gates and walk along a short tree-lined track to another gate. Go through this gate and keep close to the left-hand fence heading for the farm building in front. Go through the pedestrian gate beside the barn and then downhill to a gate beside a hollow ash tree to continue down the farm track. On a clear day this is a stand and stare moment – a timeless view across the Herefordshire Plain with the silvery Wye flowing through a patchwork of fields and farm houses. ▶ Skirt right at the farmyard gate to detour round Woolla Farm through the wood and then turn right to rejoin the farm track (SO 437 449). Note this detour around Woolla Farm is a permissive route so there is divergence between your OS map and what is on the ground.

There is a well-placed bench beside the veteran oak tree a short distance ahead.

After Woolla Farm cross a cattle grid into a large field (before Benfield Farm). As the farm track bears to the right, the Wye Valley Walk leaves the track, bearing left across the field to pass to the left of veteran ash trees. Continue downhill to the left of another ash tree and head for a central gateway into the next field. Go through the gateway and walk slightly right downhill to a gate in the right-hand corner of the field. Pass through this gate and up into the next field, hugging the boundary on the right to go through another gate very soon. Take the track uphill to the right. At the road turn left to walk down to **Bredwardine**. Stage 8 finishes at the Red Lion Hotel.

BREDWARDINE

Bredwardine is a very small village with few accommodation opportunities, including the 17th-century former coaching inn, the Red Lion Hotel, which generally serves food 12-2pm and 7pm-9pm (except Mondays). Do check in advance as there is nowhere else to find refreshments on the route between Hay and Hereford apart from Brobury House Walled Garden Café, 1km away.

THE WYE VALLEY WALK

STAGE 9
Bredwardine to Byford

Start	Red Lion Hotel, Bredwardine, SO 331 444
Finish	Byford Church, SO 397 429
Distance	7.7km (4¾ miles)
Time	2hr 20min
Ascent	80m (260ft)
Terrain	1.5km of road walking on quiet country lanes; mainly field edge paths and farm tracks through orchards
OS map	Explorer 201 Knighton & Presteigne
Refreshments	Brobury House Walled Garden Café (1km from start)
Public toilets	None on route
Public transport	Bus service 446 between Staunton-on-Wye and Hereford stops at Byford (not Sundays); bus service 447 from Bredwardine to Hereford is one early bus and one late bus Monday to Friday

An easy stage on quiet lanes at the start, visiting Kilvert's church at Bredwardine, crossing the Wye at Bredwardine Bridge and passing Brobury House Gardens. Back on the footpath at Brobury Scar, pass knarled old chestnut trees where the Wye has cut deep into the sandstone creating a 92m drop to the river below. A mile-long avenue of Scots pine and yew trees, planted in 1623, leads to Monnington Court and nearby St Mary's Church, a time-warp from the restoration of Charles II in 1679. The route then passes through extensive cider apple orchards, owned by Bulmers of Hereford, to reach Byford.

Note: The only refreshments on route between Bredwardine and Hereford are at the start of this stage at Brobury House Gardens.

Bredwardine to Monnington Court (4.6km, 1hr 15min)

From the Red Lion Hotel take the road signposted Staunton and Brobury House, passing the war memorial on the left to walk along the road for a short distance. Turn right towards St Andrew's Church.

STAGE 9 – BREDWARDINE TO BYFORD

Francis Kilvert was the vicar of Clyro and Bredwardine and is much loved for his nature writing. He kept a diary recording day-to-day events and a now lost way of life on the Welsh border. A memorial seat, under the huge yew tree in the churchyard, commemorates Francis, who died here in 1879, aged 38, just five weeks after his wedding to Elizabeth Anne Rowland. His grave is a simple white cross close to the north side of the tower. Kilvert describes a favourite walk in his diary, capturing the joy he felt walking local paths. It is the route the Wye Valley Walk follows for the next 4.8km, along Brobury Scar to Monnington Church, where Kilvert's brother-in-law was the vicar.

Turn left in front of the church, passing the Old Rectory to the right (where Kilvert lived), before going over a stile and across the field down to the road. Go over the stile and turn right to cross Brobury Bridge.

Brobury Scar (photo: Michael Mable)

THE WYE VALLEY WALK

Linking the hamlets of Bredwardine and Brobury this beautiful **bridge** is the only brick bridge on the Wye. The original 1769 bridge was rebuilt to its original plan in the 1920s following centuries of decay and flood damage. In his diary for 11 November 1878 Kilvert records how a great flood washed local residents out of their houses.

Continue along the road, going uphill and passing Brobury House Gardens.

Land which had been the vegetable gardens of Bredwardine vicarage was used in 1881 to build **Brobury House** and its terraced gardens, just two years after Kilvert's death. It's thought Kilvert planted the mulberry tree on the terrace lawn. Today the gardens focus on water features and rare trees with a walled garden adjacent to the café.

When you reach the crossroads turn right and stay on this lane until reaching a T-junction. Turn left. Ignore the first bridleway on the right. When the lane levels out at the top of the hill, branch right down a path to the right of the field gate. The path soon opens out at a place called **Brobury Scar**.

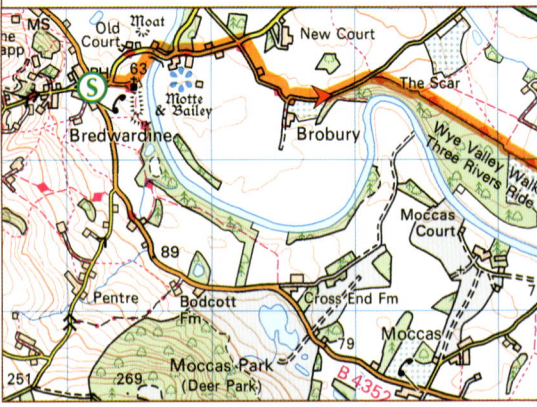

STAGE 9 – BREDWARDINE TO BYFORD

The Wye has cut deeply into the sandstone at **Brobury Scar** to create a cliff-like bluff with a steep drop down to the river below. The woodland is full of many distinctive, wonderfully shaped trees. A group of truly magnificent sweet chestnuts, which must be hundreds of years old, are so big you could hide inside them, adding to the ancient feel of this place.

Keep on the path running high above the Wye, until reaching a fork. Go left, but make sure to look to your right where the sweet chestnuts stand. Go through the gate (SO 354 444) and walk along the field edge to your right. Go through another gateway into a huge arable field, characteristic of farming on the Herefordshire Plain. (To access Dairy House Farm B&B, leave the route at the end of the second field, turning left to follow the bridleway across two fields for 0.4km.) At the end of the second field turn right through the gate onto Monnington Walk.

When James Tomkins of **Monnington Court** was elected to Parliament in 1623, he celebrated his success by planting a mile-long avenue of Scots pine and yew trees – the Monnington Walk. Some

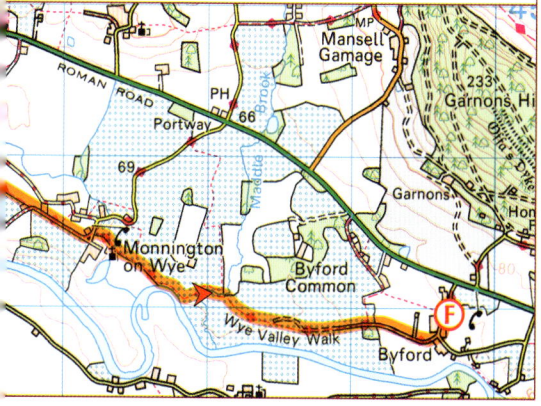

of the yew trees may be original survivors from the 17th century, but many of the Scots pines have been replaced over the centuries. Monnington Court stands at the far end of the mile.

Keep walking as the path becomes a tarmac lane. Nearing Monnington Court, just before the first sculpture, turn left. ◄

> The sculpture is by one of Britain's most prolific sculptors, Angela Conner, who lives here.

Monnington Court to Byford Church (3.1km, 1hr 5min)

Straightaway, look out for the Bulmers orchard on the right and turn right before the gate. Follow the grassy track around Monnington Court, through a gateway, passing buildings on the right to arrive at St Mary's Church in **Monnington on Wye**.

> **St Mary's Church** is a little gem, having no road access, being surrounded by water on three sides and still lit by oil lamps. Uvedale Tomkins of Monnington Court rebuilt the original 13th-century church in 1679. His grandfather, James, had been a staunch supporter of the king during the English Civil War, for which he was hung by the Parliamentarians in 1643. Such was the family's support for the king that on the restoration of Charles II, Uvedale erected a royal coat of arms to celebrate.

Follow the path through the graveyard to the left of the church and into the orchard, keeping to the right of the trees. The path keeps to the right of the orchard, briefly meeting the Wye (though hard to see in summer) before turning left away from the river, along a wide cutting in the trees.

At the Bulmers sign go straight on, over the footbridge, and turn left to walk around the edge of the orchard, keeping the hedge on your left and ignoring a gap in the hedge. At the end of this orchard, at the 'Fish with Care' sign, turn right and immediately left to join the more defined track running between the orchard on the left and a wet woodland area on the right. Follow

STAGE 9 – BREDWARDINE TO BYFORD

this track through the orchard, passing veteran oak trees. Keep straight on until the farm track reaches the tarmac lane. (To access Byford Glamping, turn right here and follow Green Lane for 0.5km.) Turn left and walk up to the church in **Byford**, which is on the right, where this stage ends. There are no facilities in Byford.

> The 600-year-old wall paintings inside the **Church of St John the Baptist** at Byford were uncovered in 1951. The painting on the south wall shows St Margaret with a book and cross. More paintings were discovered in the 1970s on the east wall, showing the Virgin Mary and St Michael.

CIDER COUNTRY

Blossom time in the Bulmers orchards

This is cider country, with more than half of the UK's cider produced in Herefordshire. Viscount Scudamore advocated cider making in Herefordshire in the 1600s. He had been ambassador at the court of King Louis XIII, and on his return to England brought home with him a collection of cider fruit from Normandy. Some of the varieties he championed, such as Foxwhelp and Redstreak, were recorded in the *Herefordshire Pomona*, a beautifully illustrated 19th-century book which you can see at the Cider Museum in Hereford. Many of the old traditional orchards, which have large apple trees, widely spaced apart and often covered in mistletoe, have been lost. Where they have been replaced it is generally with rows of intensively managed bush orchards which produce more fruit, but sadly are not beneficial to wildlife.

THE WYE VALLEY WALK

STAGE 10
Byford to Hereford

Start	Byford Church, SO 397 429
Finish	Wye Bridge, Hereford, SO 508 395
Distance	15.7km (9¾ miles)
Time	4hr 40min
Ascent	135m (445ft)
Terrain	5km stretch of fairly quiet road; field edge and riverside path; A438 is crossed twice
OS map	Explorers 189 Hereford & Ross-on-Wye, 202 Leominster & Bromyard, 201 Knighton & Presteigne
Refreshments	None on route
Public toilets	None on route
Public transport	Bus service 446 Byford to Hereford (not Sunday); bus service X15 Builth to Hereford stops at Byford Wednesdays only

Start with a visit to Byford Church to see the wall paintings uncovered in 1951. There is a very short section along the A438 and then a 5km stretch of fairly quiet road, which crosses the line of Offa's Dyke and follows a section of old Roman road past the site of Magna Castra, a Romano-British walled town. Back on footpaths, cross the A438 again to walk through orchards and fields to the pretty church at Breinton with its lychgate and links to Sir Edward Elgar. After the church, a peaceful path hugs the riverbank all the way into Hereford. Climb steps up to the old railway bridge to cross the Wye, continuing under the new road bridge to reach the 15th-century Wye Bridge.

Byford to Magnis Roman Town (4.6km, 1hr 15min)

From Byford Church follow the lane up to the A438. Turn right to walk on the verge beside the main road for a very short distance. Look out for the gatehouse on the other side of the road and cross the A438 to walk up the road to the right of it. Stay on this road for 4km, ignoring all roads to left and right and passing through the village of **Bishopstone**. At the junction for Kenchester Church pass

STAGE 10 – BYFORD TO HEREFORD

a small green on the left, with two welcome benches, overlooked by Lady Southampton's Chapel. ▶ Continue on the road and after the last house on the left the Romano British town of **Magna Castra** lies beneath the grass. A stile on the left provides access to the field.

> **Magnis Roman Town** was a small, walled, urban settlement, believed to have been the home of the Dobunni, a local British tribe. All the buildings and streets of the town are preserved as buried features in this field.

(To reach the Priory Hotel near Stretton Sugwas, leave the route, turning left straight after Magnis Roman Town along the road for 0.3km and then branching right to follow the Three Rivers Ride for 3km. To access local shop and takeaway in Credenhill, stay on the road for 1km.)

Magnis Roman Town to Lower Breinton Church (6.9km, 2hr 10min)

The route continues along the road, heading towards the A438. Soon, where the road bears right, keep left to go through a gate into a field and follow the hedge on the left through two fields. (These fields are liable to flooding.) Go through the gate on the left, just before a house, which leads to a gravel track winding between houses, then a tarmac road up to the A438. Turn left and walk along the pavement in **Sugwas Pool** for 0.2km.

In 1830, influenced by Wesley, Baroness Southampton set up two chapels with schools to improve conditions for the poor in Kenchester and nearby Breinton.

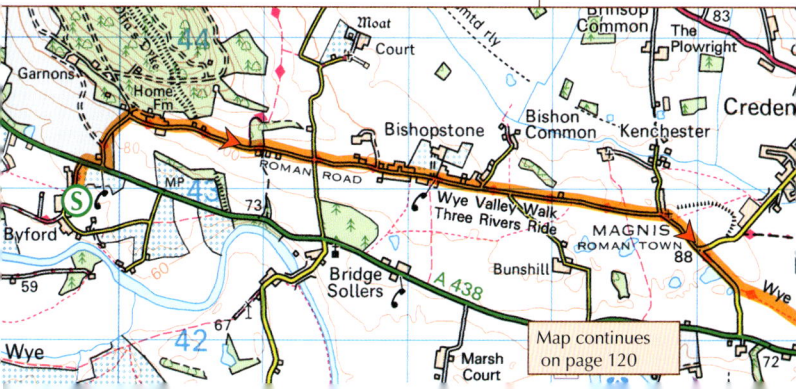

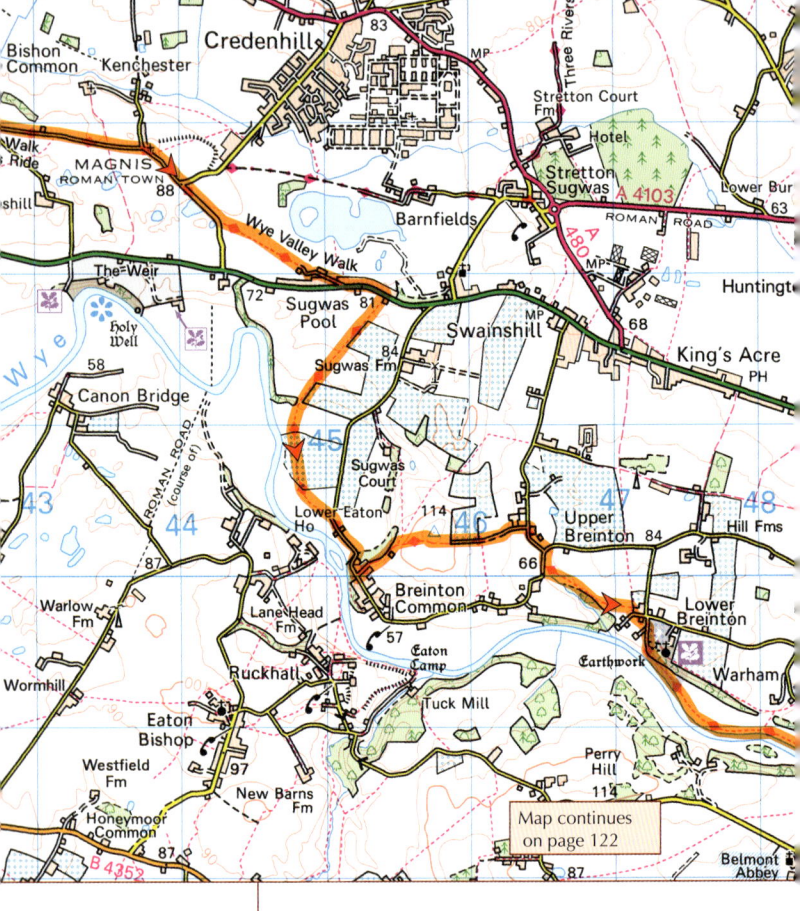

Nearing the end of the village look out for the post box and, just before it, turn right across the A438 to go down a field footpath, keeping to the hedge on the left until reaching a farm track. Keep straight on along the track until it bears right. The route continues beside the hedge to the left, through the orchard. At the far corner of the orchard keep left through a gap in the hedge and continue beside the hedge on your left through another field. At the end of this field go through a gate and straight on past a small copse of trees on the right.

STAGE 10 – BYFORD TO HEREFORD

Head straight across the field to a small gap in the hedge and go over a stile. Look for a waymarker on the end of the row of fruit trees and walk straight ahead between the trees. Turn left at the end of the row and keep going until you come to a stile on the right, just before a line of mistletoe-clad poplar trees. Go over the stile into a field and bear diagonally left across the field, looking for a tiny gap in the hedge and another stile. Turn right along the road soon arriving in **Breinton Common**.

When the road levels out turn left in front of Eaton View along a bridleway between the houses, and then climb along a gravel track which becomes a narrow path after Park View. Go through a gate and keep right following the hedge. Near the top of the field look back to enjoy the expansive view behind you. Turn right through a gate and go straight across the field. ▶ Go through a gate onto a track which leads downhill, coming out in **Upper Breinton**. Turn right. At the next junction turn right signposted Breinton Common. Look out for the footbridge (SO 465 400) on the left, cross it and go up steps to a gate. Bear right across the field to the top right-hand corner through a gateway and follow the hedge through the second field. At the corner of the field turn right through a kissing gate and along a path to the road. Cross the road to go through a metal gate and along a grassy path through a small orchard, keeping left at the fork. At the road turn right down the road passing the church at **Lower Breinton** on your left.

> The city of Hereford and the Malvern Hills are visible from here on a clear day.

St Michael's is a Norman church dating to around 1200, which was completely rebuilt in the 1860s. Nearby earthworks are thought to be the remains of a medieval, moated manor house built in the 12th century, with a possible deserted medieval village in the undulating ground in the orchard. The church is one of many sites in the area associated with the English composer Sir Edward Elgar. His friend Canon Charles Vincent Gorton is buried in the churchyard, with a line of music from Elgar's oratorio *The Apostles* on his grave. Another grave of

THE WYE VALLEY WALK

interest is that of Herbert Gatliff, the son of a Rector of Breinton, who was buried in the family grave overlooking the Wye in 1977. Gatliff was a top civil servant in the Treasury and loved long-distance walking and youth hostelling. Disappointed to find there were no hostels in the Outer Hebrides he set up the Gatliff Trust, funding hostels on the Scottish islands and furthering his interests in the enjoyment and care of the countryside by young people.

Lower Breinton Church to Hereford (4.2km, 1hr 15min)

Walk through the car park to a gate on the right and a path down to the riverside, which you now follow all the way into Hereford. ◄ After a while the Broomy Hill Water Tower will come into view in the distance.

> Belmont Abbey is visible on the opposite bank, a community of about 30 monks who follow the 6th-century Rule of St Benedict.

The Wye is a source of drinking water for many of the communities living along its banks, and a visit to the **Waterworks Museum** (open Tuesdays 11am–4pm) brings the story of drinking water to life.

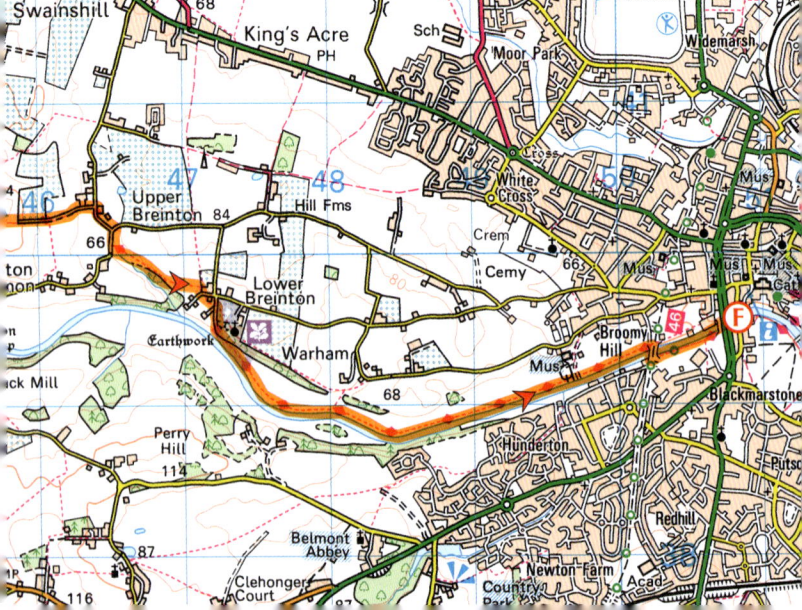

STAGE 10 – BYFORD TO HEREFORD

Hereford Cathedral

When you reach the playing fields keep right along the riverbank. At the old railway bridge turn left to immediately go up steps to reach the top of the bridge. Turn right to cross the river (or if you want to visit the Cider Museum or city centre go left along the railway track cycleway) and at the end of the bridge turn left down the steps. At the bottom of the steps follow the riverside path passing under the road bridge. The riverbanks here were the focus of trade in Hereford for many hundreds of years.

RIVER TRADE

The Wye Navigation Acts passed in the 17th century created 100 miles of navigation rights from Hay-on-Wye through Hereford down to the tidal Wye. Wharves lined the riverbank here with weekly market boats departing for Bristol. Trows had to be hauled over rapids, by gangs of 'bow hauliers', to reach the city. Today the Wye is one of the few rivers in the UK where these traditional rights to navigate remain, mainly used by canoeists and paddle boarders.

THE WYE VALLEY WALK

Continue into **Hereford** until reaching the Wye Bridge, built around 1490, making it the oldest bridge on the Wye and where this stage ends. To visit the cathedral and city centre attractions and facilities cross the bridge.

HEREFORD

Hereford is a lovely little city, with a low-key, country feel. On clear days the Black Mountains seem to be right on the doorstep.

A place of worship since 696, Hereford Cathedral was rebuilt in the early 12th century in the Norman/Romanesque style. By the end of the 12th century it had become an important national centre of learning. Chaining books was an effective security system and Hereford's unique 17th-century chained library is the largest to survive with all its chains, rods and locks intact. Look out for the work of Thomas Denny in the tiny Audley Chapel, where stained glass windows celebrate the work of Thomas Traherne, the Herefordshire poet, born in 1636, who loved nature and the natural landscape.

Peaceful gardens around the cathedral

Another treasure of the medieval world, the Hereford Mappa Mundi is also to be found in the cathedral. Created around 1300, over 500 drawings detail the known world, giving a fascinating insight into how scholars interpreted the world at that time.

Nowadays, the city's food and drink scene is based on local produce from the Herefordshire countryside. Head over to Hereford's Museum of Cider for tastings and tours, housed in the original factory where Bulmers began making cider in 1888. For shopping, head over to Church Street, close to the cathedral, which has delightful independent shops, art galleries and food stops. Trekitt should be able to solve any outdoor kit or walking supplies issues. For lovers of the Jacobean period a visit to the Black and White House Museum will reward with rare wall paintings and fine English oak furniture. Find arts and evening entertainment at the Courtyard Arts Centre and, if you're lucky, the Three Choirs Festival which rotates annually between Hereford, Gloucester and Worcester may be in town! There's also a mainline railway station and bus services to Hay-on-Wye and Ross-on Wye.

Lots of independent shops in the city

STAGE 11
Hereford to Fownhope

Start	Wye Bridge, Hereford SO 508 395
Finish	Fownhope, 700m from village centre SO 581 351
Distance	11km (6¾ miles)
Time	4hr
Ascent	80m (260ft)
Terrain	Urban route leaving Hereford; field-edge and level riverside paths; hilly after Mordiford
OS map	Explorer 189 Hereford & Ross-on-Wye
Refreshments	Bunch of Carrots in Hampton Bishop (5min off route), Moon at Mordiford (2min off route), Green Man and New Inn at Fownhope (700m from end of Stage 11)
Public toilets	None between Hereford and Fownhope
Public transport	Bus service 453/454 runs between Hereford and Fownhope (no service Sundays)

From the Wye Bridge a riverside path leads through Bishops Meadow to the Victoria suspension bridge to cross the Wye. The walk then follows urban routes out of Hereford, leaving the city behind and joining a footpath which runs close to the Wye across the flood plain to Hampton Bishop. Crossing the B4224 the path follows the flood defence banks to the River Lugg at Mordiford, where you enter the Wye Valley National Landscape, an area of outstanding natural beauty. Leaving the river behind, the path climbs through traditional orchards and crosses secluded fields between Mordiford and Fownhope. If you wish to visit Fownhope at the end of this stage, take the road just south of Nupend Farm, which leads down to the village 700m away.

Note: When the river is in flood, paths beside the Wye may be closed. Check water levels at: https://check-for-flooding.service.gov.uk/station/4017. The route on your OS map may differ from the route described, which avoids stretches which flood regularly.

STAGE 11 – HEREFORD TO FOWNHOPE

Hereford to Mordiford Mill (8.4km, 2hr 10min)

Start beside the Saracens Head pub by the old Wye Bridge. Take the path between the pub and the river heading downstream through Bishops Meadow until reaching the next bridge. Turn left to cross the elegant Victoria suspension bridge. The Wye Valley Walk continues straight on to reach Mill Street. Go straight across to walk along Nelson Street. Turn right to walk along Green Street (Bartonsham Meadows nature reserve is straight ahead) then turn left along Park Street. When Park Street ends cross the B4224 and turn right to walk under the railway bridge. Continue on the pavement along Eign Road, which later becomes Hampton Park Road, for 1.5km. Pass the composer Edward Elgar's home on the left, which is marked by a blue plaque. ▶

As the houses thin out, look out for Sudbury Avenue on the left and use the pedestrian crossing to cross the B4224. Take the path between the houses, crossing another road, going through a gate and following the path, with houses to your right, down to a kissing gate.

Keep right along the field edge, with the river soon on the right. After 0.7km the footpath leaves the riverbank to cut diagonally left across the middle of the field (aim to go to left of right-hand pylon) and up onto The Stank flood defence embankment. (Sometimes this path may be covered in crops so continue along the field edge until you can spot a way through the crops.) Turn right through the gate after the concrete bridge to walk along the flood defence. At the gateway turn left down the steps. Turn right to walk carefully along the B4224 for a very short distance to the layby and bus stop. ▶ At the end of the layby turn left through a kissing gate into a field. Head straight across the field to the right-hand corner and go through the gate to walk between the houses. Turn left to walk along the road for 0.8km.

One of Elgar's most creative periods was between 1904 and 1911, while he was living in Hereford.

The Bunch of Carrots pub is a little further along this road if you need a refreshment stop.

The Wye Valley Walk

If you would like to visit the Norman church of **St Andrews**, which has an unusual black and white timbered belfry on top of the Norman tower, continue on the road for a few minutes. It's likely Elgar played the organ here when he was working on compositions, apparently inspired by the nearby view from Mordiford Bridge.

When the road bears right turn left to walk up to a cattle pen and take a narrow path on the right, through a kissing gate. Follow the raised track on top of the flood defences for approximately 1.2km all the way to

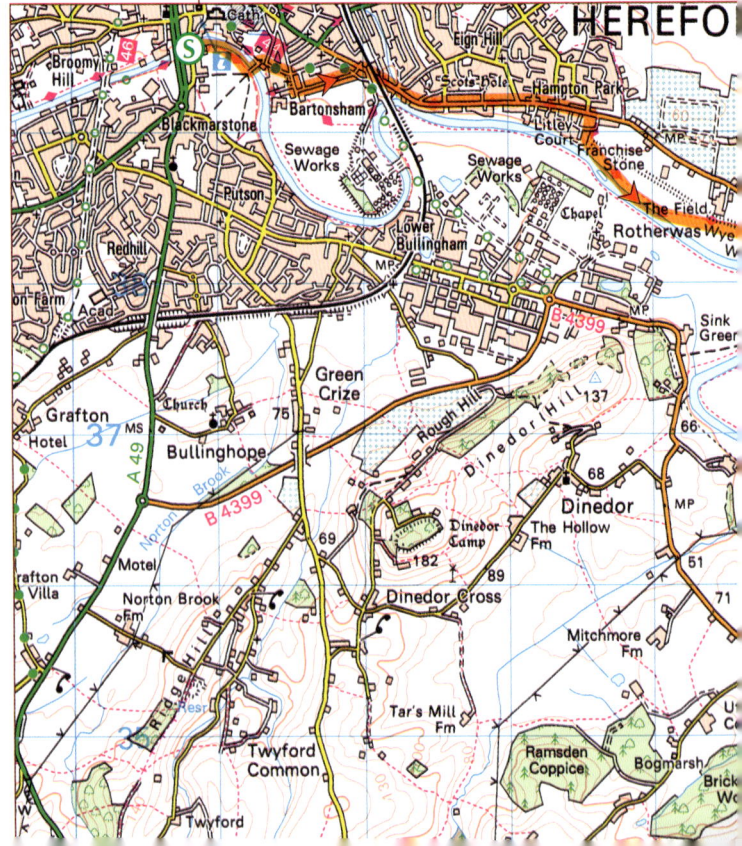

STAGE 11 – HEREFORD TO FOWNHOPE

Mordiford, passing through several gates. Just before Mordiford Bridge go down the flood bank to the right, through gates and then up to the road (SO 568 375). Turn left to cross the bridge over the River Lugg, keeping to the left.

Pass the Grade II* listed Holy Rood Church, with its ancient preaching cross and exterior stone carvings, on the left. Then cross the road to walk along the pavement on the right, turning right immediately before the old post office. Cross the bridge and turn left straight away. At the B4224 go straight across to walk in front of the three-storey Mordiford Mill, a watermill with an overshot wheel.

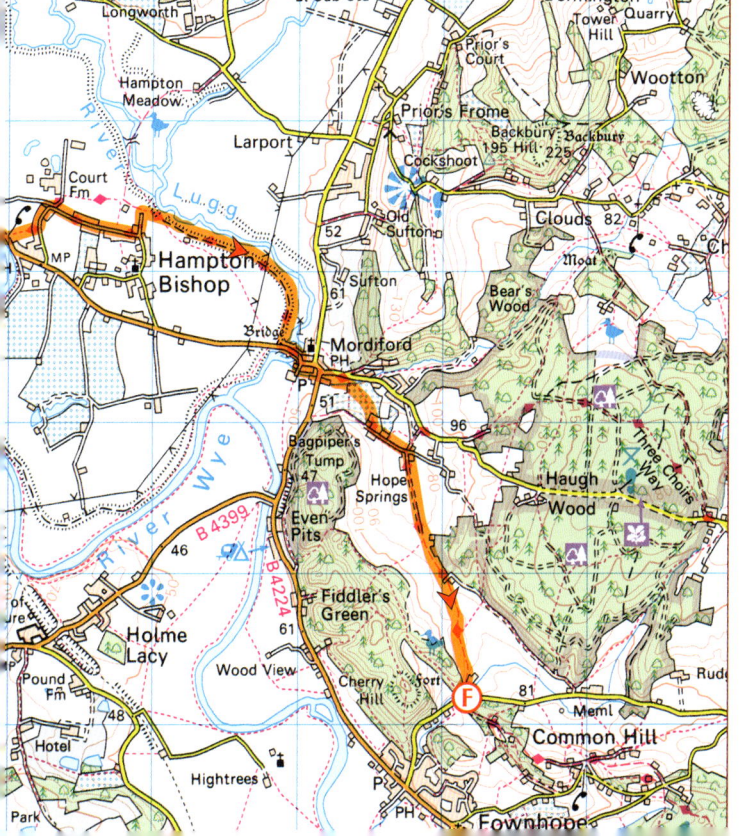

THE WYE VALLEY WALK

MORDIFORD

You are now in the Wye Valley National Landscape. The final 83km of the Wye Valley Walk runs through this area of outstanding natural beauty, which was designated in 1971. Mordiford grew up at the confluence of the Wye and Lugg and parts of the bridge date to the 1350s, making it the oldest surviving bridge in Herefordshire. Trows carried cargo along the Lugg, with the most unusual cargo to travel through this bridge's arches surely the bells of Leominster Priory, which in 1756 arrived afloat in Chepstow to be recast. Navigation on the Lugg ended around 1829.

Until the 19th century a huge green dragon, which had three pairs of wings and four pairs of legs, was painted on an exterior wall of Mordiford Church. It was probably inspired by the many dragon legends which have been part of local folklore for centuries. One of them, the story of a local girl who befriended a dragon, has been brought to life in a series of wooden sculptures on the Dragon's Trail around the village.

Mordiford Mill to Fownhope junction (2.6km, 50min)

Go through the gate and stay on the track, through another gate, keeping to the left of the hedge. Go through a kissing gate in the corner of the field and over a bridge beside a dragon! Walk to the left of the hedge immediately in front of you, up through the left-hand orchard, following the hedge on your right.

Sheep grazing a traditional orchard at Mordiford

STAGE 11 – HEREFORD TO FOWNHOPE

TRADITIONAL ORCHARDS AND NOBLE CHAFER BEETLES

A very rare noble chafer beetle found in a Mordiford orchard (photo: Ellie Bagget)

The noble chafer beetle is a gorgeous metallic-green beetle found in traditional orchards. It is classed as nationally scarce in Great Britain. Traditional orchards are an important feature of the Wye Valley National Landscape, but the number of orchards reduced dramatically during the 20th century, leading to the loss of the noble chafer beetle's primary habitat – the deadwood at the heart of decaying trees, which also provides a safe place for the beetle's larvae to live. A project to reverse the decline of the noble chafer, led by the Wye Valley National Landscape team, started with a beetle 'census', to find out where the noble chafers are. Traps with a synthesised pheromone lure, specially developed to attract noble chafers, were hung in local orchards. This orchard was one of a very few sites where a noble chafer beetle was actually found and therefore habitat boxes have been installed to create new homes for chafers.

When the orchard ends go through a gate and up the path. Turn left at the track to walk along a tarmac lane past the intriguingly named Bagpiper Cottage at **Bagpiper's Tump**. At the Bullbox converted farm buildings turn right to walk between the buildings, keeping left of the barns as the road becomes a gravel track. Stay on this track, skirting the edge of **Haugh Wood**.

Keep straight on when you reach a lone house on the left at Citterdine.

Go through the gate and ignore the track to the right, keeping straight on into a large field. Follow the hedge on the left, keeping to the right of an oak tree and walking parallel to the pylons. Pass another hidden-away house on the left as you go through an old gateway into the next field. Follow the hedge on your left, go through the next gateway and then head across the field towards the far right-hand corner. Join a path which passes large oak trees and then becomes a stony track leading down to a field gate at Nupend Farm. Go through the gate, and straight on to immediately bear left over the brook and walk up to the road where this stage ends. For local services in Fownhope turn right to walk 700m down into the village.

OAK APPLE DAY

Fownhope is home to the traditional Heart of Oak Club Walk, which takes place each year on the Saturday closest to Oak Apple Day, 29 May. Fownhope Heart of Oak Friendly Society was formed in 1876 to provide payments for members (mainly agricultural workers) if they fell on hard times. The society held a celebration each year with a club walk, a church service and a dinner with speeches in the Green Man Inn. Fownhope Heart of Oak Society has preserved the club walk tradition even though it no longer has the financial obligations of a friendly society. On the morning of the walk an oak bough is cut from the woods and decorated with red, white and blue ribbons. This leads the parade followed by the society banner, the band and members of the Fownhope Community carrying club sticks decorated with flowers. The original Heart of Oak Friendly Society banner can be viewed in St Mary's Church, which also has one of the finest examples in the country of a 12th-century Norman tympanum.

FOWNHOPE

The attractive village of Fownhope has three shops (Pritchard's Butchers, West End Stores and the Shop @ Coo Corner), two pubs (New Inn and Green Man) and a small number of places to stay.

STAGE 12
Fownhope to Ross-on-Wye

Start	Fownhope, 700m from village centre SO 581 351
Finish	Ross-on-Wye, outside the Hope and Anchor Inn SO 596 242
Distance	17.2km (10¾ miles)
Time	5hr 30min
Ascent	275m (900ft)
Terrain	Short stretches along quiet country lanes; field edges and riverside paths
OS map	Explorer 189 Hereford & Ross-on-Wye
Refreshments	New Inn and Green Man pubs in Fownhope (700m off route); small farm shop and self-serve café at Townsend Farm, Brampton Abbots (1km off route)
Public toilets	None between Fownhope and Ross. Composting accessible toilet at Townsend Farm (1km off route)
Public transport	Bus service 453 between Hereford and Fownhope (not Sundays); bus service 454 Hereford to Woolhope (one bus daily, not Sundays)

From Fownhope the route is a mixture of woodland and farmland, passing through Common Hill Nature Reserve and Lea and Paget's Wood, Sites of Special Scientific Interest. The walk crosses farmland to join the Wye at How Caple along a pleasant riverside path. A 3km section of narrow tarmac lane is followed passing the hamlet of Hole-in-the-Wall and Foy suspension bridge. Soon after the bridge a mostly level footpath leads all the way to Ross, including a short section of old railway track. In summer look out for sand martins nesting on the opposite bank near Backney Common. The path continues past Ross Rowing Club to reach the Hope & Anchor pub.

Note: The farmland between How Caple and Ross-on-Wye can be very muddy in wet weather and flood when the Wye breaches its banks.

Fownhope to Capler Lodge (4.8km, 1hr 45min)

From the end of Stage 11 at Nupend Farm, cross the road and immediately go left uphill along the track. Keep straight on at a junction of tracks by a house on the left. After the stables take the left fork and go straight ahead uphill, ignoring paths off to the side, along a wooded track. This widens after a house and the view opens up to the left towards Haugh Wood. ◄ Continue on the track, passing a house called Morning Star, to a junction locally known as Common Hill Fiveways, where a sign points to the **Tom Spring memorial**.

> The wood is home to 600 different species of butterflies and moths, including the pearl-bordered fritillary, the wood white and the drab loper moth.

Local lad **Tom Spring** was a bare-knuckle boxer who was the heavy weight champion of all England in the 1820s. A short detour will take you to his memorial, which stands alongside a traditional apple press with a vertical millstone (pulled by a donkey) and a handy picnic table.

Another sign points downhill to two redundant buildings which have recently found a new lease of life. The **pump house** was erected in 1916 to provide water for the local community but now acts as a wet weather shelter for walkers. The old red **phone box** has become a local information kiosk.

Go straight across, taking the left-hand fork up a tree-lined lane. To the left is North Meadow, part of **Common Hill Nature Reserve**.

It is well worth walking through the traditional meadow of **Common Hill Nature Reserve** to enjoy the views, and in late spring and summer the wildflowers and butterflies. This reserve lies on the north slope of a limestone ridge where thin, free draining and nutrient-poor soil produces a spectacular grassland including cowslips and marjoram. Some of these plants will only grow on land which has never been ploughed or improved with fertilisers and herbicides.

STAGE 12 – FOWNHOPE TO ROSS-ON-WYE

A gate on the left accesses this limestone grassland meadow and you can follow a small path uphill through the field, passing a bench, and then rejoining the Wye Valley Walk a little further along, opposite Monument Hill and Round's Meadow (also part of the reserve). Stay on the enclosed track and at the tarmac lane turn right, and immediately left, through a gate in front of Common Hill Farm and over a stile. The view to the right opens out. Walk downhill to the left along the field edge, through a gateway and into Lea and Paget's Wood (SO 599 340).

Lea and Paget's Wood is one of the finest ancient, semi-natural broadleaved woodlands within the Wye Valley National Landscape and a Site of Special Scientific Interest managed by Herefordshire Wildlife Trust. There are many ancient woodland indicator species, as the extra light created through coppicing has encouraged a variety of plants to thrive, with a spectacular show of bluebells, primroses, wood anemone and yellow archangel in spring.

Traditional limestone grassland meadows at Common Hill Nature Reserve

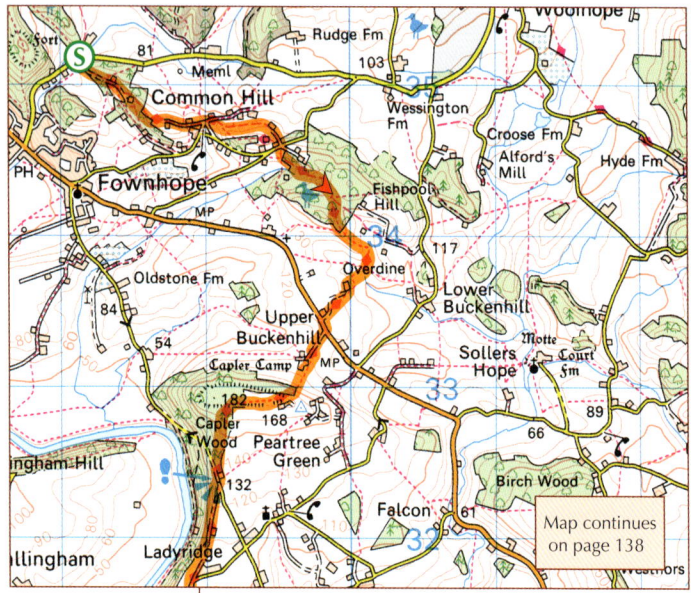

Look out for the tops of a pair of limekilns on the left as you enter the wood. Stay on the main track through the woodland. At the junction of paths take the right-hand fork, leading to a kissing gate into a field, passing a bench and information sign. Follow the hedge on the right downhill and through a gate/stile, then follow the fence down and through a gate beside an oak tree. Head for a small metal gate with a curved top, just to the left of a farm gate, in the right-hand corner of the field. Follow the hedge downhill and then through a gap in the hedge into another field. Go through a gateway (the actual route here may differ from your OS map) and walk uphill between the farm buildings and apple trees at **Overdine**. Go through a kissing gate and walk straight across the field to a gate on the right near to a house at Hill Crest. Go through the gate and turn left to reach the B4224.

Turn left at the main road and take care while walking a short distance along the B4224 to a turning on the

Stage 12 – Fownhope to Ross-on-Wye

right for Caplor. Turn right and walk up the lane. Turn left into the yard and straight away turn right to walk to the left of the main office building. Head uphill keeping to the left of the buildings and house. Go through a kissing gate and continue up past the glamping pods at Caplor Farm. Go through a gate and up steep steps and over a stile. Turn right and head uphill. The route passes to the right of the stone barn but there is a bench with lovely views to the left of the barn. Walk through the defences of **Capler Camp**.

> The Iron Age hillfort of **Capler Camp** commands a strategic position overlooking the Wye Valley, with views to Mayhill and Chase Hill above Ross-on-Wye. It is oval in shape and has a double set of defensive ramparts on its southern side, but only a single rampart on its steeper northern side. You can make out the rampart and ditch defences as you walk through the site. The camp was occupied from around 500BC until the late 2nd or 3rd century AD. Tradition has it a British chieftain is buried here.

Go through a gate on the left into **Capler Wood** and then, after a gap in the field hedge, turn left downhill through pine trees to meet a forest track. Turn left and descend to the road. Turn left to reach a picnic bench at the **viewpoint** at Capler Lodge.

Capler Lodge to Foy Bridge (7km, 2hr)

Straight after the viewpoint turn right down a gravel track, through a gateway to pass West Cottage and another group of houses. At the tarmac lane turn right and immediately left down a footpath at **Brinkley Hill**. Keep to the field edge on the right. At the corner of the field turn left along a track between two fields, ignoring paths to either side. Turn right at the road and at the T-junction keep straight on uphill through the hamlet of **Totnor**. Turn right at Rose Cottage (where the road bears left) onto a footpath leading down to a gate. Cross the field, going

The Wye Valley Walk

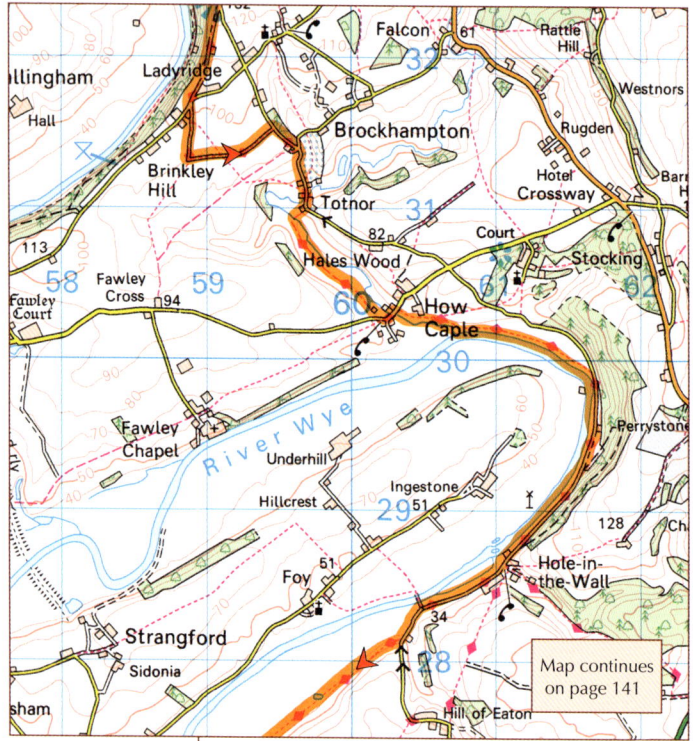

slightly to the right, to a footbridge over a pretty stream, and through a gate into another field. Turn left and walk the length of this very long field, eventually heading to a gate in the far right-hand corner. Go through this gate, along a track and through another gate, then passing a house on your left. Walk through the garden down to the road. (Please note, the phone box shown on the OS map at Garroway House has been removed.)

Turn left downhill and soon, just after White House Farm (home to White House Glamping camping and cabins), go over a bridge and turn right along a fenced off

STAGE 12 – FOWNHOPE TO ROSS-ON-WYE

footpath, which becomes a field edge path, first following a stream on your right and then the Wye.

It's good to see the river for the first time on this stage, especially as this stretch to Hole-in-the-Wall is so pretty. Keep to the riverbank and eventually go over a footbridge and walk up to the road. Turn right to walk past Lyndor Cottages and through the hamlet of **Hole-in-the-Wall**.

There are several suggestions regarding the origin of the unusual place name **Hole-in-the-Wall**. It may have derived from Thurlestane, mentioned in the Doomsday Book and meaning 'hole stone'. Perhaps it was the name of a pub, which literally had a hole in the wall to serve customers? On the left, just before the cattle grid, is the former Anchor and Can, which served people using the nearby Foy ferry as well as the men working the Wye trows up and down the river.

Approaching Hole-in-the-Wall (photo: Emma Drabble)

Wheelchair ramblers enjoying the view to Backney Common from Townsend Farm

Continue along the road and look out for Foy Bridge on the right.

You can cross this bridge and take the riverbank path to the left to visit **Foy Church**. Standing on top of a small cliff of old red sandstone overlooking the Wye, this location fits the idea of isolation sought by the early Celtic saints. The church was originally dedicated to St Tvyoi or Ffwy (probably a disciple of St Dyfrig). The Normans didn't recognise Celtic saints and the dedication was changed to Saint Foy (old French for faith) and later St Mary. Inside the church on a carved screen is the hedgehog symbol of the ancient Welsh kingdom of Ergyng. The original Foy footbridge was constructed in the 19th century through public subscription, to allow residents on the English side of the river to attend this church on the Welsh side. However, the bridge also made it easier to visit the pub on the English side!

Foy Bridge to Backney Common view (2.2km, 45min)
Soon after the bridge, at Orchard Cottage, turn right along a hidden, shady footpath. Go through the gate into the field and walk along the right-hand edge of the field (with views to **Foy Church** to the right). Go through a kissing gate and along the farm track. At the end of this field go through another kissing gate, up steps and

Stage 12 – Fownhope to Ross-on-Wye

REGENERATIVE AGRICULTURE AT TOWNSEND FARM

Over the last 20 years or so flooding has eroded 20m from the opposite riverbank, providing habitat for sand martins who build their nests by digging small tunnels into the bank. Their numbers have increased dramatically here in recent years. It's a good place to spot other river birds such as kingfishers and cormorants. At Townsend Farm Ben Taylor-Davies and his family are showcasing regenerative agriculture, moving away from intensive farming to methods which regenerate their soils for a more sustainable future. You can follow waymarked walks around the farm where information panels explain what is happening, view the massive New Horizons mural and pop into the small honesty farm shop and self-service café.

through Monks Grove wood. Turn left out of the wood to walk along the edge of the woodland. When it ends keep straight on across the field towards poplar trees, passing a pond to your right. Follow the track beside the hedge up to a junction with a farm track. (Leave the route here and turn left to access Townsend Farm (1km), where there is a small self-service farm shop, café, toilet and micro brewery, and glamping. Glamping at Mad Dogs and Vintage Vans in Brampton Abbots is also accessed via this farm track, which passes The Cot.) The Wye Valley Walk turns right and enters an expansive field on Townsend Farm, where just to your right there is a small bench looking across the Wye to Backney Common.

THE WYE VALLEY WALK

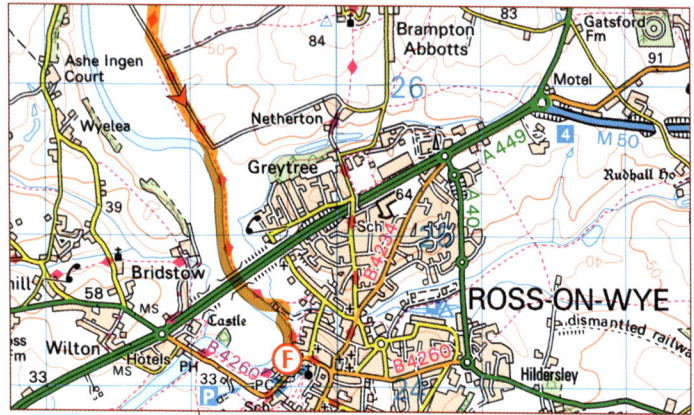

Backney Common view to Ross-on-Wye (3km, 1hr)
The Wye Valley Walk follows the left-hand field edge, passing to the left of the oak tree. At the end of the field climb up steps to the old railway line.

> The **Hereford, Ross & Gloucester Railway** operated between 1855 and 1964. The meandering Wye needed to be crossed four times on this section between Ross and Hereford, presenting some tough engineering solutions.

THE WYE TOUR

The height of fashion 250 years ago was a boat tour down the Wye Valley to view the romantic ruins and picturesque landscape. Tourists came to be inspired by the scenery, to paint, sketch and write. They embarked on the Tour at the town dock, the area in front of the Hope and Anchor. At least eight boats operated from here, with the pub hiring out boats fitted with 'every suitable convenience' and boatmen who were, reassuringly, 'well skilled in navigation'. Tour boats were designed with cushioned seats arranged around a table so passengers could sketch or write during the voyage.

STAGE 12 – FOWNHOPE TO ROSS-ON-WYE

Walenty Pytel's amazing swan sculpture in Ross-on-Wye (photo: Gemma Kate Wood)

Turn left along the railway line and when the track ends turn right down to the riverbank. Turn left to walk beside the river, under Bridstow Bridge and, just before the rowing club, left over the footbridge. Walk through the car parking area and turn right over another footbridge. Continue on the riverside, passing the Walenty Pytel sculptures.

This stage ends in **Ross-on-Wye** when you reach the Hope and Anchor pub on the left.

ROSS-ON-WYE

Ross-on-Wye is a lively town with many independent shops, galleries and antique shops and a good selection of places to eat, drink and stay. The Phoenix Theatre offers music, theatre and cinema screenings, the Corn Exchange live music, jazz evenings and comedy nights, and outdoor concerts are held at the Bandstand on Wye Street with Bands in the Park on summer Sundays. Tourist information can be found at Made in Ross at the Market Hall, Truffles Delicatessen on High Street and Ross-on-Wye Town Council on High Street. Local produce includes award-winning cider and perry from Ross-on-Wye Cider & Perry Company, award-winning still and sparkling English wines from Wythall Estate Vineyard and traditional Brut cuvee sparkling wine from Castle Brook Vineyard.

THE WYE VALLEY WALK

STAGE 13

Ross-on-Wye to Kerne Bridge

Start	Ross-on-Wye, outside the Hope & Anchor Inn SO 596 242
Finish	Kerne Bridge car park, adjacent to Bishopswood Village Hall SO 581 198
Distance	8.7km (5½ miles)
Time	3hr
Ascent	375m (1230ft)
Terrain	Urban walking leaving Ross-on-Wye; much of route through woodland with several steep climbs
OS map	Explorers OS14 Wye Valley & Forest of Dean, 189 Hereford & Ross-on-Wye
Refreshments	None on route. Paddle Café at Kerne Bridge Canoe Launch (summer months only, check opening times at www.thepaddlecafekernebridge.com), Inn on the Wye, Hen & Dot Café at Flanesford Priory (not open year-round, check opening times at www.henanddot.co.uk), Goodrich Castle tearooms (1km from end of stage)
Public toilets	Toilets in Ross-on-Wye and at Bishopswood Village Hall
Public transport	Bus service 746 between Ross-on-Wye and Kerne Bridge (not Sundays); bus service 34 between Ross-On-Wye and Monmouth daily

Leaving Ross along urban roads, this stage is a pleasant mix of woodland and farmland walking. There is a steep climb out of Ross to woodland and a further climb up to Chase Hill Iron Age hillfort. An intricate network of small paths and lanes is followed around Leys Hill and descending to Kerne Bridge.

The 'Man of Ross' was John Kyrle, a 17th-century philanthropist remembered for the good work he undertook in the town.

Ross-on-Wye to Coughton (4.7km, 1hr 30min)

Facing the Hope and Anchor, follow in the footsteps of earlier Wye tourists by taking the steps to the left of the pub up to the road. Turn left uphill along Wye Street. Pass the leaping salmon sculpture, by internationally renowned sculptor Walenty Pytel, which stands in front of the Man of Ross pub. ◄

STAGE 13 – ROSS-ON-WYE TO KERNE BRIDGE

Cross the road to walk along High Street for a short distance. If you would like to explore the town and its independent shops and vintage shopping trail continue along High Street. You can see the Market House straight ahead.

King Stephen granted Ross-on-Wye the right to hold a market in the 12th century. The **Market House** is one of the oldest buildings in the town centre. Around 1650 the Duchess of Somerset paid for its construction using local red sandstone and Forest of Dean oak. Today the upper floor of the Market House is home to Made in Ross, which showcases local art and crafts and also provides tourist information.

Just after the King's Head Hotel turn right along Church Street. Very soon on the left are the Tudor almshouses, built of local red sandstone. Turn right here, up the curved steps and walk diagonally towards St Mary's Church, passing the Plague Cross. ▶ To the right you can see the Gazebo Tower and Royal Hotel.

The cross remembers the 315 citizens of Ross who died in the outbreak of plague in 1637 and were buried at night without coffins.

Ross-on-Wye, birthplace of British tourism (photo: Drew Buckley)

THE WYE VALLEY WALK

The **Gazebo Tower** was built in 1833 as a folly, providing a viewing point over the horseshoe bend in the Wye. Mock gothic town walls were constructed at the same time as part of a new road building scheme, undoubtedly in part a response to the number of tourists arriving in the town to take the Wye Tour. Opposite the tower is **the Royal Hotel**, built in 1837 on the site of an old bishop's palace, catering for the tourists with its commanding views.

Walk past the entrance to St Mary's Church and around the corner of the church.

'Rhosan' in Welsh or Celtic means a promontory and **St Mary's Church** stands on the promontory which is thought to have given Ross its name. Most of the present church was built between 1280 and its dedication in 1316. Inside are many memorials including the grave of John Kyrle.

LAND OF THE HEDGEHOG

The hedgehog has special significance in Ross-on-Wye and the surrounding area. This area was part of the ancient Welsh kingdom of Ergyng, which came to be known as Archenfield in the 9th century, meaning 'Land of Hedgehogs'. Today the hedgehog is the emblem of Ross-on-Wye. Start looking and you will find this favourite little animal depicted in wood, stone, stained glass and paint, in churches and on other buildings in the area, including St Mary's Church where hedgehog icons adorn family crests dating back to the 17th century.

Keep right to go through the impressive stone gateway into The Prospect, hinting at the elegance of this place in the past. Follow the path around the park, which has far-reaching views across the horseshoe bend of the Wye, stretching from Brampton Abbotts to the Welsh mountains. It's interesting to see the direction of Hay-on-Wye and Hereford, passed earlier on this walk, on the stone plinth adjacent to the Beacon, which is lit for celebratory events.

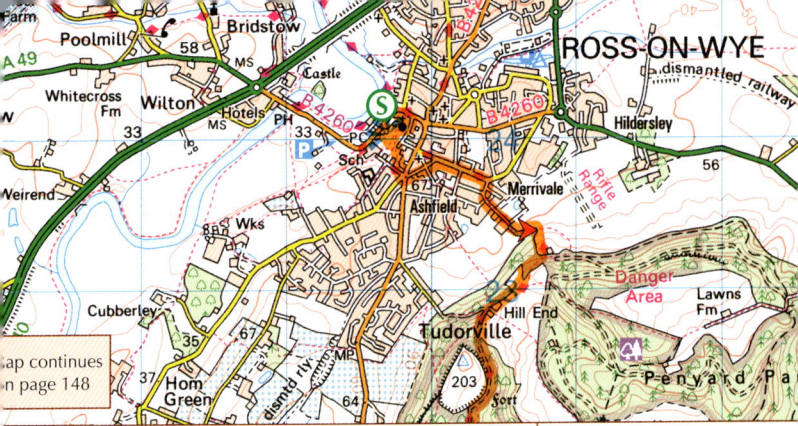

John Kyrle (the Man of Ross) leased the land here in 1697 to create a **public garden and clifftop walkway**. Kyrle designed a square garden with four entrances, a fountain and a sundial. In 1837 the owner of the Royal Hotel partitioned part of The Prospect for hotel guests to use. This caused widespread protest, as local people believed The Prospect belonged to the town. Riots and protests continued until 1870 when Thomas Blake paid for the land to be transferred to the town forever.

The **Museum Without Walls** is Ross-on-Wye's virtual museum, using augmented reality to bring historic sites around the town back to life. Download the Museum Without Walls app on your phone to view the fountain which once stood here.

Exit The Prospect through the ornate Kyrle's Gateway, with the date 1700 carved into the stonework. Turn left and keep straight on to reach the entrance gates to the churchyard. Turn right to walk across Crossfield car park to the left, passing the bowling club and tennis courts. At the B4234 you need to go straight across and head down the residential road in front of you. It's called Kent Avenue, but there is no sign for it at this end of the street. Use the pedestrian crossing to the right to cross the road and then walk down Kent Avenue. At the bottom of Kent

THE WYE VALLEY WALK

Avenue turn right by Ashdean to walk along Alton Street. At the end of Alton Street turn right down Penyard Lane, walking past the industrial estate, over the cycle crossing and passing Alton Court, a 17th-century timber-framed building which is now the headquarters of PGL.

> In 1957 Peter Gordon Lawrence decided he wanted to share his passion for the outdoors with young adults, by leading canoe trips through stunning scenery and camping under the stars. Looking for a river which had free navigation rights he found the Wye and so it was that Ross-on-Wye became the base for **PGL Voyages** (later nicknamed 'Parents Get Lost'). PGL has become Britain's leading operator of adventure courses for schools and children's outdoor activity holidays, introducing millions of youngsters to the great outdoors.

MERIVALE WOOD NATURE RESERVE

This Hereford Wildlife Trust reserve is part of a much larger area of ancient woodland, providing habitats for woodland birds, such as blackcap, marsh tit and woodland butterflies. A medieval deer park covered these woods, which were used as hunting grounds by the bishops of Hereford, who had a bishop's palace in Ross. Wardens guarded against poachers but in 1354 the bishop of Hereford's warden, Walter Moton, was tried for carrying off 1300 deer.

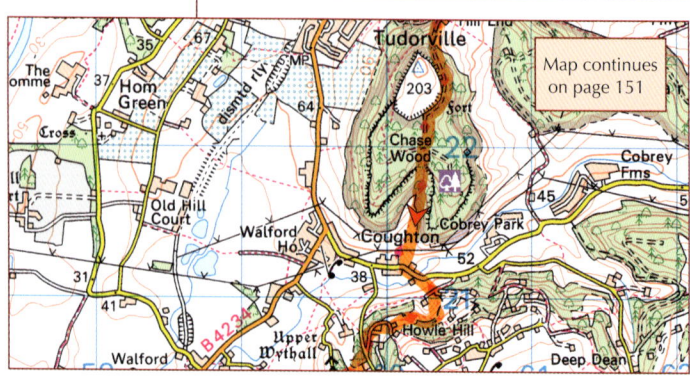

Map continues on page 151

When the road ends take the path on the left through a kissing gate through a wood. Keep left to go through a kissing gate into a field. Turn right to follow the field boundary uphill, through a gate into the wood. Turn right to go through a second gate straightaway through Merrivale Wood Nature Reserve.

When the path leaves the wood, turn right, go through the kissing gate and keep left through woodland. Keep left at the fork, through a kissing gate. Walk straight ahead, ignoring side paths and passing the forestry barrier. Here the track forks at the phone mast, keep left to climb steadily uphill. As the path widens around Chase Hill stay on the main track, and when the track bears left you can see humps and bumps of the Iron Age hillfort to your right.

> At 201m the **Chase Wood Iron Age Hillfort** had commanding views over the River Wye and surrounding land. Covering 19 acres, it was occupied in the 5th and 4th centuries BC, perhaps up to the time of the Roman invasion. There is no public access to the fort.

Stay on the main track until four tracks converge at a large conifer in the middle of the track, take the second exit (easy to miss as it's a very small path) downhill, through fir trees. The path descends quite steeply and down a set of steps. When you reach the field turn left to go down the path on the left of the field fence (this route may not be shown on your OS map). Go through the kissing gate and straight on heading to a gate to the left of houses, passing a carved millstone, and through more gates to reach the road at **Coughton**. ▶

The Wye Valley Farm Gate Shop is on the left, which may, depending on season, be selling local rhubarb or asparagus.

Coughton to Kerne Bridge (4km, 1hr 30min)

Turn left to walk along the road and after a short distance turn right after Coughton Mill, through a kissing gate and keep to left field boundary up to the gate. Cross the lane to Craig Farm and go through another gate onto a path which climbs through mature trees. The path bears left across the field to a gateway, through another gate and

The Wye Valley Walk

> Wythall Estate opens their wine garden on selected dates during spring and summer and offer vineyard tours and wine tasting, and self-catering accommodation.

then bears right up to a gravel track. Turn right and at the next junction turn right, winding around scattered houses. Keep straight on where two lines of concrete become gravel, soon emerging onto a road. Go straight across, following the path down through woodland, a kissing gate, down a steep fenced off path, over a stream and into the vineyard at **Upper Wythall**. ◄

Keep to the right of the vines, climbing steeply uphill over stiles and steps which lead around a house. Bear right after the house, down to the road and turn left across the road, taking the footpath immediately on the right for **Walford**.

> The village of **Walford** derives its name from 'Wales-ford', where the old road from Ross forded the river into Wales.

Go down a wooded stretch on a narrow path. At the junction keep left to go straight on as the path widens on the woodland edge. At a house called The Rock the path joins a lane coming up from the right in front of a stone building. Keep straight on at nearby junction of paths, ignoring paths on either side. Go straight on where power lines cross overhead ignoring paths to left. Go through a gateway, passing Tump House on the left. At the junction turn left, climbing up a lane. Keep straight on at Cherry Tree Cottage along a steep section, with lovely, coppiced trees lining the path. When you reach two houses, do not bear left, go straight on opposite the sign for Rose Cottage, between the two properties. Very soon turn right down a footpath between fields and through two gates. Go straight over in front of Ravenshurst sign and then left down steps and around the house down to the road at Kerne Cottage. Turn right. Cross the road at the junction and go through a gap in the hedge, in the bus stop layby, into the car park beside Bishopswood Village Hall (to the right) where this stage ends. To the left is Kerne Bridge Canoe Launch, where there is a refreshment van, The Paddle Café, during summer months.

The Wye was once considered to be one of the finest **salmon** rivers in the country. Robert Pashley, who lived at Kerne Lodge, was the most successful salmon fisherman, catching over 10,000 salmon! In recent years the salmon's decline in the Wye has been dramatic. The Wye and Usk Foundation works to conserve and protect salmon and other indigenous species on the Wye and Usk. Find out about their work at www.wyeuskfoundation.org.

Find accommodation and food at The Inn on the Wye, 5min before Kerne Bridge. Cross Kerne Bridge for Flanesford Priory and the Hostelrie at Goodrich (1km).

Leys Hill and Kerne Bridge (photo: Adam Fisher)

Dragon's breath at Symonds Yat (Stage 14; photo: Adam Fisher)

The Wye Valley Walk

STAGE 14
Kerne Bridge to Symonds Yat

Start	Kerne Bridge car park, adjacent to Bishopswood Village Hall, SO 581 189
Finish	Saracens Head, Symonds Yat East, adjacent to hand ferry, SO 561 158
Distance	11km (6¾ miles)
Time	3hr
Ascent	250m (820ft)
Terrain	Riverside path; steep ascent to Symonds Yat Rock; steep descent to Symonds Yat East
OS map	Explorer OL14 Wye Valley & Forest of Dean
Refreshments	Inn on the Wye (2min off route); Hen & Dot Café at Flanesford Priory, Kerne Bridge (seasonal; 2min off route); Goodrich Castle tearooms (1km off route); The Hostelrie at Goodrich (1km off route); Wye Valley Youth Hostel (on route, check opening times), Symonds Yat Rock Café
Public toilets	Bishopswood Village Hall, Symonds Yat Rock and Symonds Yat East
Public transport	Bus service 35 between Ross-on-Wye and Monmouth stops at Kerne Bridge. Bus service 746 runs between Kerne Bridge and Ross-on-Wye (not Sundays)

Cross the Wye at Kerne Bridge, with the silhouette of Goodrich Castle on the hill above. It's a level path on the west bank of the Wye all the way to Welsh Bicknor, running through woodland and then across floodplain meadows. The old Lydbrook railway bridge takes you over the Wye to the east bank, where the path continues through very peaceful riverside fields. With steep slopes on both sides and superb views up to the limestone cliffs of Coldwell Rocks and Symonds Yat Rock, this is a spectacular section. The path follows the route of the old Wye Valley Railway beneath the cliffs before leaving the river for a steep ascent to Symonds Yat Rock and the most famous view on the Walk. A steep zigzag path takes you down to Symonds Yat East.

STAGE 14 – KERNE BRIDGE TO SYMONDS YAT

Goodrich Castle (photo: Gemma Kate Wood)

Note: Your OS map may show a low-level route around Huntsham Hill rather than the official route up to Symonds Yat Rock.

Kerne Bridge to Stowfield Bridge, Lydbrook (6km, 1hr 30min)

From the Kerne Bridge car park walk to the right towards Bishopswood Village Hall, where a path leaves the car park, passing to the left of the hall, along the route of the old Wye Valley Railway line. Follow this path. ▶

Don't forget to collect your passport stamp from the Inn on the Wye to your right just before you cross Kerne Bridge.

Surveyed by Isambard Kingdom Brunel in 1851, the 13-mile **Wye Valley Railway** line between Ross-on-Wye and Monmouth took eight years to build, opened in 1873 and closed in 1965.

The Wye Valley Walk

Pass the old Kerne Bridge Station, which is now a house, to your left. At the B4229 turn left and cross the road to walk along the narrow pavement on Kerne Bridge. In front of you is **Flanesford Priory** and on the horizon Goodrich Castle.

Opened in 1828, **Kerne Bridge** was built to accommodate Wye trows, with a stone tow path constructed under the archway nearest to the right bank. Flanesford Priory, an Augustinian Priory, mentioned in the Domesday Book, was established in 1346 by Sir Richard John Talbot, Lord of Goodrich Castle. Goodrich Castle dates from the 11th century, soon after the Norman invasion, and is one of the best-preserved medieval castles in England. It gave the Marcher lords control of the important river crossing below. Held by both sides at different times during the Civil War, it was a massive, locally made cannon known as 'Roaring Meg' which led to the castle's ultimate surrender to the Parliamentarian forces during a siege in 1646.

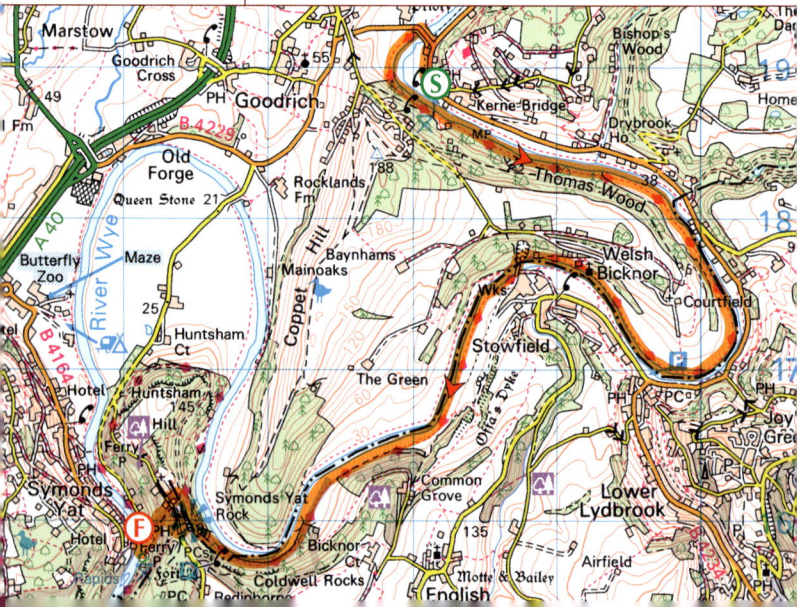

If you would like to visit **Goodrich Castle** you can make a short detour by continuing along the roadside, taking the path on the left up to and over the bridge, turning right to walk into Goodrich village and then turn right up to the castle.

At the end of Kerne Bridge cross the road again and take the steps down into the field, to follow the riverside path. The path climbs steps up into woodland. Ignore track off to right. You will soon see the canoe launch on the opposite bank beside the remains of the railway bridge. Keep to the riverbank at the house. The path can be slippery after rain with slides down to the river. The path leaves **Thomas Wood** entering the riverside fields through a gate (where you could pretend to be a horse and take the jump option). Continue alongside the Wye through floodplain meadows and keep left along the riverbank where the track forks. The path follows the Wye as it makes a sweeping loop and the steeple of Welsh Bicknor Church will become visible in the distance alongside the old Victorian rectory, now the Wye Valley Youth Hostel. Look to the right to see the buildings of **Courtfield** on the hill to your right.

Courtfield was the childhood home of King Henry V. He was born at Monmouth Castle in 1387, but taken to Courtfield, the home of his cousin Lady Mary Montague, for safekeeping, where he lived until 1394.

Beavers were introduced to the Greathough Brook, which flows into the Wye near Lydbrook, in 2018. In 2023 the first beaver kits were born. The beavers have built dams, helping to restore the ecosystem of the brook, store water and slow flows. Since 2018 storm water rates have reduced by 30 per cent according to research by the University of Exeter, helping to lessen the impact of flooding.

Go over two stiles to walk along the left edge of the camping field. Stay on the path and at the apple trees in front of the church keep left, taking a small path to follow the riverbank. Don't head up to the youth hostel (unless open for refreshments or staying there).

As the name '**Welsh Bicknor**' suggests, this land on the west bank of the Wye was once in Wales. The Book of Llandaff mentions a church in this area which was the Bishop of Llandaff's seat from the late 6th to early 10th century. At this time the bishopric was Welsh, and remained Welsh-speaking until the 17th century. With apple trees and an ancient cider press just outside the churchyard this is a lovely peaceful place.

Stay on the riverside path until reaching **Stowfield** railway bridge, where the path curves up to the right to access the bridge.

Welsh Bicknor Church

STAGE 14 – KERNE BRIDGE TO SYMONDS YAT

Stowfield Bridge to Symonds Yat East (5km, 1hr 30min)

Cross the bridge and take the steps down, turning left to walk under the bridge. You soon pass a slipway (note the sign!) and fisherman's hut. The path goes through a gate and into a long field following the riverbank.

> The buildings of the former **Lydbrook Cable Works** can be seen to the left. This was a huge cable manufacturing operation for much of the 20th century. During World War 1, 650 munition workers, mainly women, were employed, producing 15,000 miles of cable for field telephones used on the Western Front. In World War 2 the fine wire used in the heated jackets worn by fighter pilots and bomber crew, was manufactured here.

At the end of this long field go left through the kissing gate and up steps to join the old railway line. Turn right, go through a gate and follow the old railway line. The view opens out after about 1 km. ▶ In front of you are the towering cliffs of **Coldwell Rocks**, where Wye Tourists disembarked from their tour boats to climb up to Symonds Yat Rock.

If the scenery looks familiar that's because this area featured in the film Shadowlands about CS Lewis, (author of The Chronicles of Narnia).

COLDWELL ROCKS

The carboniferous limestone cliffs at Symonds Yat are a magnet for birds of prey, including the peregrine falcon, which nests on Coldwell Rocks. A telescope observation point at Yat Rock allows visitors to view the nest site and find out more about peregrine falcons. You can watch the peregrines while they hunt and raise their young between April and August. There are around 1750 breeding pairs in the UK now. Other birds of prey such as the goshawk, sparrowhawk and common buzzard can also be seen here. Sometimes ospreys, on their spring and autumn migrations, stop off, attracted by the river where kingfishers, sand martins, swifts, swallows and house martins all nest.

Nearing Coldwell Rocks (photo: Gemma Kate Wood)

When the field ends, go through the gate and continue along a forestry track for just under 1km. The path starts to climb after passing a track on the left leading up to a house. Now look out for a flight of steps on the left, which you take climbing on a narrow path until reaching a junction and a signpost to 'Yat Rock ¼ mile'. Turn right for Yat Rock, passing alongside a house on your left and turning left when you reach a parking area and two strips of concrete track. At the road go straight across to walk along a path signed for Yat Rock. Turn left at the next junction signed Yat Rock and continue up a steep section, which comes out near the Symonds Yat Rock Café, a log cabin with outdoor tables. To reach the viewpoint, go left over the wooden walkway bridge up to **Symonds Yat Rock**. Your OS map may show an alternate low-level route around Huntsham Hill rather than the official route up the steep climb to Symonds Yat Rock.

The Wye flows in a massive loop hundreds of feet below **Symonds Yat Rock**, creating one of the most iconic views on the Wye Valley Walk. It's a view which has been delighting visitors for hundreds of years. Wye Tourists would have climbed up the steep path while their tour boats continued along the Wye, to meet their passengers at Symonds Yat East. Today, as well as the grand river scenery, viewing the peregrine falcons is part of the attraction of Yat Rock.

STAGE 14 – KERNE BRIDGE TO SYMONDS YAT

After taking in the view and enjoying a drink at the café, retrace your route down the steep wooded section to the junction of paths by the signpost. Turn left signposted for Symonds Yat East. Turn left at the next junction, in front of The Chalet, a characterful wooden house which featured in the Netflix hit *Sex Education*, which was filmed in the lower Wye Valley. Unless the river is very low you will soon hear the rapids. At the bottom turn right to walk along the road and reach the **Saracens Head Inn** on the right and the hand ferry on the left, where this stage ends. Collect your passport stamp at the Saracens Head.

In the 19th century there were at least twenty-five **ferries** between Chepstow and Ross-on-Wye, linking communities living on either side of the river. They carried cargo, foot passengers and even animals across the Wye. Most of these ferries were hand powered, where the ferry man pulled the boat to the other bank using an overhead cable. This traditional hand ferry is the only surviving one still working regularly on the Wye.

The hand ferry saves a five-mile road trip to Symonds Yat West (photo: Emma Drabble)

SYMONDS YAT

There are three parts to Symonds Yat. Enjoy the famous viewpoint from Symonds Yat Rock. Facilities here include car parking, toilets and a log cabin café. A steep zigzag footpath leads down from Yat Rock to the riverside settlement of Symonds Yat East (on the east side of the Wye). Accommodation on this side of the river includes the Saracens Head, Royal Lodge, Wye Rapids B&B, Garth Cottage and The Chalet. WyeDean Canoe and Activity Centre and Kingfisher Cruises are also on this side of the river. There are public toilets opposite the Saracens Head and two pay and display car parks. The more scattered settlement of Symonds Yat West, on the other side of the Wye, can be reached on foot by taking the hand-operated rope ferry, run by the Saracen's Head Inn, across the river. Attractions in Symonds Yat West include the Wye Valley Butterfly Zoo, the Amazing Hedge Puzzle, and short river cruises leaving from Symonds Yat West Leisure Park. Accommodation includes River Wye Caravan and Camping, Sterrett's Caravan Park, Ye Olde Ferrie Inn, Paddocks Hotel, Old Court Hotel and The Rapids Cottage.

STAGE 15
Symonds Yat to Monmouth

Start	Saracens Head, Symonds Yat East, adjacent to the hand ferry SO 561 158
Finish	Monmouth SO 511 127
Distance	8.8km (5½ miles)
Time	2hr
Ascent	90m (295ft)
Terrain	Mostly level terrain following old railway line; riverside fields and woods; narrow in places, muddy in wet weather
OS map	Explorer OL14 Wye Valley & Forest of Dean
Refreshments	Biblins Lodge Tea Garden (seasonal)
Public toilets	Symonds Yat East, Biblins Youth Campsite (seasonal)
Public transport	None

Weaving in and out of Wales, the border is crossed four times on this mostly level stage. The path follows the east bank of the Wye from Symonds Yat East, along the former railway track (now the Peregrine Path cycle way). Half-way to Monmouth, the path crosses a much-loved pedestrian suspension bridge at Biblins, continuing on the west bank of the Wye underneath limestone cliffs known as the Severn Sisters and King Arthur's Cave. Passing the largely hidden mansion of Wyastone Leys, where the valley widens out, riverside fields then lead down to Monmouth, passing a pretty little riverside church at Dixton.

The wooded Wye Gorge below Symonds Yat (photo: Adam Fisher)

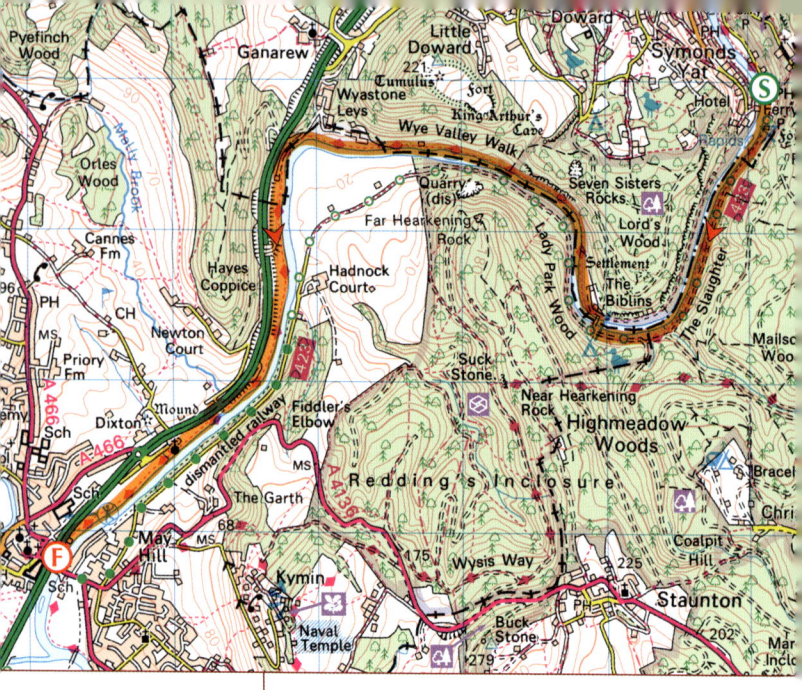

From the Saracens Head Inn, turn left to walk along the road with the river to your right. Go through the car park and onto a gravel track. This is the Peregrine Path, a cycle way which runs all the way to Monmouth, but you only follow it as far as the Biblins suspension bridge.

The **rapids** on the right formed from a collapsed weir. The weir diverted water from the river to fill a forge pond at the New Weir **ironworks**, on the opposite bank. Operating from the 1590s to the 1800s these ironworks were one of many interconnected metal-making sites along the Wye. Following the Navigation Acts a lock had to be provided by the owner of the ironworks so that boats could pass through freely. Today the rapids are a popular training site for canoeists.

STAGE 15 – SYMONDS YAT TO MONMOUTH

Continue along the Peregrine Path which follows the route of the former Wye Valley Railway line.

Imagine steaming through here in days gone by. The **Wye Valley Railway** ran between Ross and Symonds Yat from 1873 to 1959. The arrival of the railway saw Symonds Yat become one of the most popular destinations along the Wye.

LADY PARK WOOD

This National Nature Reserve of ancient woodland is a unique experiment in neglect and is definitely off limits! It has been completely abandoned, on purpose, since 1945. It is a long-term study area to see how woodland develops naturally when there is no human interference. Species that depend on light, open conditions (achieved through coppicing and thinning) are not faring so well here, while fungi, insects and mosses are thriving in the shady conditions. The Aborealists, a group of professional artists, have also been studying this wood, creating a fascinating book, *Art Meets Ecology: The Arborealists at Lady Park Wood*, illustrating how natural woodland works.

After 2km, just before you reach the **Biblins bridge** (SO549 144), is **Lady Park Wood** on the left.

Turn right to cross the bridge to **Biblins Youth Campsite** (a Forestry Commission site managed by Woodcraft Folk). Turn left off the bridge and keep to the left of the camping field, passing the seasonal Biblins Lodge Tea Garden on the right. Leave the field to follow the riverside path through woodland. ▶

Look out for evidence of limestone quarrying to the right, while high above you are steep limestone cliffs including the Seven Sisters Rocks and King Arthur's Cave.

BUTTERFLIES ON THE DOWARD

In the 19th and early 20th centuries the Doward was well known among butterfly collectors, who arrived at Symonds Yat on special excursion trains. Local boys caught purple emperors and other rare butterflies and sold them to the visitors. Today there are around 30 indigenous species of butterfly on the Doward hills including colonies of wood white, pearl-bordered fritillary, small heath, silver-washed fritillary, grizzled skipper and dingy skipper. The rare purple emperor butterfly is found very occasionally.

THE WYE VALLEY WALK

KING ARTHUR'S CAVE AND THE HYENA'S DEN

When hyena remains were found in a limestone cave on the Doward they attracted the attention of the Reverend William Symonds, a well-known Victorian geologist. A local man called Slippery Jem, who lived with his wife in a nearby cavern, helped Symonds locate the cave, which soon came to be known as the Hyena's Den. Symonds removed huge amounts of debris using dynamite to blast concrete-like stalagmite deposits from the cave floor. Underneath he discovered bones from lion, hyena, woolly rhinoceros, cave bear and mammoth. In the last Ice Age this area was on the edge of the tundra and the cave provided shelter for humans too. Slippery Jem, who boasted he had lived in his cave for 30 years, was following a long tradition of cave dwellers. Jem and his wife Betsy were probably the last cave dwellers on the Doward. Betsy picked wild strawberries and sold them to tourists at Symonds Yat. Jem made fur slippers from the skin of animals he trapped (hence the name Slipper) to sell as souvenirs.

If you wish to explore, a very steep path on the right will take you up to King Arthur's Cave.

These gates probably date back to Victorian ironmaster Richard Blakemore's time at Wyastone Leys, which you will soon reach.

Go through a large metal gate and before the second metal gate keep left on the track close to the river. (A sign says 'Little Doward – Woodland Trust' just before the path on the right.) ◄ Pass the rapids around Hadnock Island and a house on the right. When the path emerges into a field keep to the left along the riverbank. Hidden behind the trees to the right is **Wyastone Leys** and above is Doward Hill.

Richard Blakemore, a wealthy Victorian ironmaster, moved to Little Doward in 1820 with grand ideas. As well as rebuilding his house, **Wyastone Leys**, he set about creating a new picturesque landscape around it, blasting through cliffs to form landscaped walks and carriage drives, which cut straight through the ramparts of an ancient hillfort. You can still see the holes in the rock face where the dynamite was placed. The crowning glory of Blakemore's estate was a 70-foot, six-sided iron viewing tower, which visitors were allowed to climb on Sunday evenings. Compared to the Iron Age hillfort, which has survived for 2000 years, Blakemore's folly lasted for less than a century.

STAGE 15 – SYMONDS YAT TO MONMOUTH

Stay on the riverside path to leave the Wyastone estate. The path climbs up through woodland (ignore track to right) and past another house to the right. Keep left beside the river at the end of the garden. The path now passes through woodland below the A449 as you cross into Wales again. Leave the woods through a gate and continue across the fields until reachingw a waymarker sign to the right, which takes you through two gates to cross the Malley Brook and back into another field. Follow the path across two footbridges and then pass through **Dixton** churchyard.

The first mention of a **church** here, called Llan Tydwg, is in AD735, in the Book of Llandaff. It was referred to as 'Hennlann', meaning 'old church' in Welsh, suggesting there had been a church here for many years before. It was probably destroyed by the Welsh prince, Gruffydd ap Llywelyn, in 1055, when he led a raid up the Wye to Hereford, devastating many riverside settlements. The church was probably rebuilt soon after and re-dedicated to St Peter. Today the parish straddles the border between England and Wales and parish records illustrate the battles for control between the dioceses of Llandaff (in Wales) and Hereford (in England). A ferry used to cross the river here and steps leading down to the river are the only reminder that churchgoers alighted here for services. The vicar rowed over

A flood marker inside St Peter's records the depth of the 1947 flood, which was way above head height

from the vicarage on the east bank too. St Peter's water meadow location has its disadvantages, with 1.8m floods not uncommon.

There is one more footbridge to cross before arriving at Monmouth Rowing Club. Note, the flood gates on the underpass can be closed at short notice at times of high water levels. If leaving a vehicle here check predicted water levels: https://riverlevels.uk/wye-monmouth-community-monmouth. This stage finishes at the Wye Bridge a little further along the riverbank. If you wish to visit **Monmouth**, take the underpass before the traffic lights and walk into town.

MONMOUTH

The most recent archeological excavations in Monmouth date back 3800 years to the Bronze Age, with the unearthing of a prehistoric boat-building site on the edge of a 'lost' lake which covered much of where Monmouth stands today. The Romans established a garrison here called Blestium. The Normans built a castle in the 11th century, controlling the crossings of the Wye and Monnow. It was here that King Henry V (of Battle of Agincourt fame) was born in 1386 or 1387. The unusual gatehouse bridge over the Monnow was constructed in the 13th century, one of only three surviving fortified bridges in Europe. Monmouth's Shire Hall was the scene of one of the most infamous trials in British history when John Frost and other Chartists were tried for their involvement in the Chartist Rising in Newport in 1839. Frost and two others were found guilty of high treason and sentenced to death. Queen Victoria intervened and they were deported to Van Diemen's Land (modern Tasmania). All the demands of the Chartists were eventually achieved, except annual parliaments. Today you can explore the courtroom and the cells where the Chartists were held. The Castle and Regimental Museum, tucked away beside the ruins of Monmouth Castle, tells the story of the Royal Monmouthshire Royal Engineers (summer only).

Monmouth has everything you might need ranging from a doctor to a Waitrose store! Pedestrianised Church Street has interesting independent shops including jewellery makers and book shops. The town has plenty of places to eat and drink and a good range of accommodation. For evening entertainment, the historic Savoy Theatre hosts live shows and films, or you might be able to catch a performance at the nearby Blake Theatre.

STAGE 16
Monmouth to Tintern

Start	Wye Bridge, Monmouth SO 511 127
Finish	Tintern Abbey SO 532 001
Distance	18.7km (11½ miles)
Time	5hr 30min
Ascent	400m (1315ft)
Terrain	Riverside paths though fields; short verge section of A466; old railway line; steep ascent to Pen-y-fan; quiet lanes, woodland tracks; steep descent to Brockweir; village path beside the A466 through Tintern
OS map	Explorer OL14 Wye Valley & Forest of Dean
Refreshments	Boat Inn and Bell Inn in Redbrook, Redbrook Village Stores; The Whitebrook (Michelin restaurant with rooms, 1km off route, booking advised); Old Station Tintern (seasonal); pubs, cafes, restaurants in Tintern
Public toilets	Old Station Tintern (seasonal, during opening hours) and Tintern Abbey
Public transport	Bus service 69 runs between Monmouth, Tintern and Chepstow

The penultimate stage takes you into the heavily wooded gorge of the Wye Valley National Landscape. Cross the Wye at Monmouth to walk along riverside fields and back into England at the former industrial village of Redbrook. Cross the railway bridge to return to Wales for the final time, then follow a riverside path and old railway line to Whitebrook, once a centre for paper making. A steep climb up narrow, stone-walled paths brings you to the hamlet of Pen-y-fan and then along the Duchess's Ride to the seasonal waterfall at Cleddon. Woodland paths high above the Wye eventually descend to the former port of Brockweir on the tidal section of the river. A short walk along the old railway line brings you to nostalgic Old Station Tintern. The final approach to Tintern is along fields beside the river and through the village to majestic Tintern Abbey.

The Wye Valley Walk

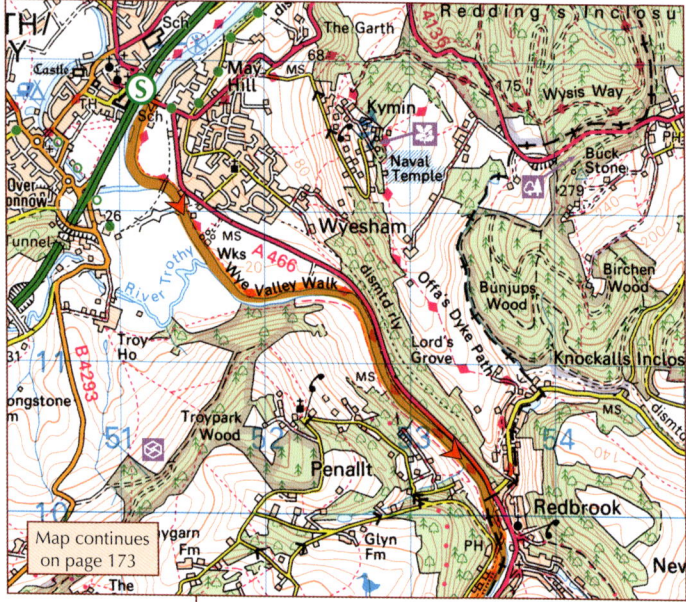

Monmouth to Redbrook (4.5km, 1hr 10min)
Walk over the Wye Bridge and at the end of the bridge turn right across the A466 to walk through the sports complex car park and to the right of the building. Take the path through a gate marked 'Old Railway Viaduct 650m'.

> This riverside area used to be a **shipbuilder's yard**. Disaster struck in 1825 as the 211-ton *Monmouth*, built here, was launched. She lurched sideways, throwing people into the river. Two young boys drowned. She was built for merchants in Bristol, voyaging to the West Indies in the 1830s and 1840s, but was lost off Cuba in 1852. Monmouth had a long tradition of building trows and boats, but ships this size needed flood water and high tides to reach the open seas of the Severn Estuary.

STAGE 16 – MONMOUTH TO TINTERN

Monmouth's Shire Hall where the Chartists were sentenced to death in 1840

Follow the riverside path around the sports field, under the old metal railway bridge and then under the remains of a stone railway viaduct, after which the path becomes narrow with drops down to the river. Go through a gate to walk across the Monmouthshire Show Society's showground, following the path beside the river. (If an event is taking place be sure to keep to the path.)

The hill to your left is the **Kymin**, which at 250m has far reaching views across the Usk Valley. On its summit the Monmouth Picnic Club constructed the Round House, a circular banqueting house, in 1794. Guests were instructed on how to observe the views in the correctly picturesque manner.

Leave the showground fields through a gate into a wooded section, where the path winds above the river and can be slippery in wet conditions. Keep straight on through a gate, passing the water monitoring station (look out for bat boxes here) and continue beside the Wye. Go through a gate which takes you up to the A466. Turn right to walk, with caution, a short distance along the verge and into England. Turn right opposite Bush House and follow the path running behind a house and alongside a fence. Just before the railway bridge take the steps up into the picnic area next to the playing field.

Redbrook has a village shop and post office, two pubs and accommodation options. There is a nice riverside area with seats just in front of the shop.

Redbrook to Duchess Ride viewpoint (6km, 2hr)

Turn right and then turn right again down the slope to the footpath that runs alongside the old railway bridge to cross the Wye back into Wales for the last time. At the end of the bridge, turn right towards the **Boat Inn** (a popular local watering hole) and walk underneath the railway bridge to your right, following the riverside path for approximately 800m. Just after the fishermen's chalet turn right up to the old railway line.

> A hard quartz conglomerate rock, known locally as 'puddingstone', outcrops in this area between Penallt and Llandogo. This rock was excellent for making the **millstones** used in cider and perry production and evidence of this industry can be found in Prisk Wood. Many millstones were loaded onto trows and transported downriver. When water levels are low you may spot some of the stones which, quite literally, missed the boat while being loaded.

If you prefer, it is possible to continue along the path by the river for a further 2km until it joins the old railway line.

At the railway line, turn left to walk along the track to **Whitebrook**. ◀

At the forestry barrier turn right to join the road and turn right to pass Tump Farm. (Stay on this road to access The Whitebrook Michelin-star restaurant with rooms (1km off route) and Highlands accommodation and camping at New Mills (3km off route).)

STAGE 16 – MONMOUTH TO TINTERN

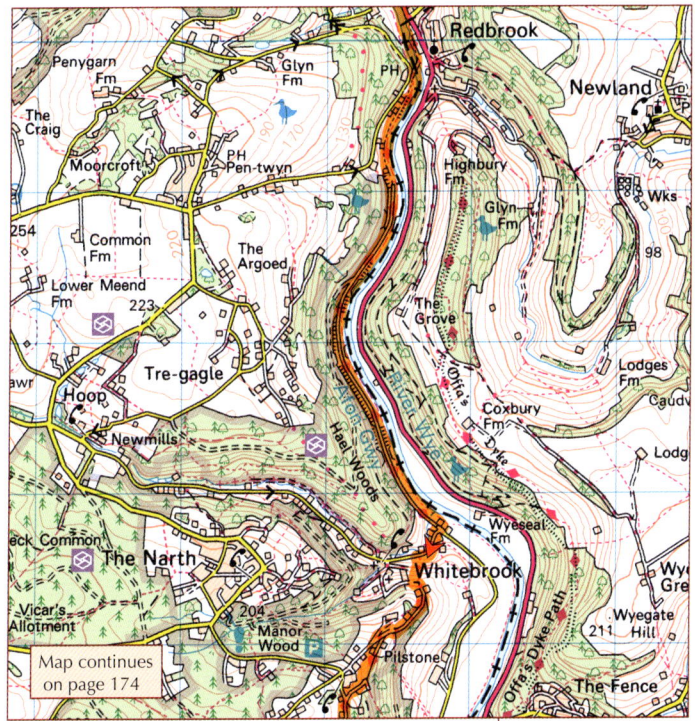

REDBROOK INDUSTRIAL HISTORY

In the 1680s, a local man, John Coster, experimented with new ways of smelting copper using coal rather than charcoal, revolutionising Britain's copper smelting industry. The English Copper Company established works here in 1692 and, securing contracts from the Mint, stamped out the blanks for copper coins, becoming the government's main supplier. Redbrook soon became Britain's copper capital, but the impact of this heavy industry on the village was profound, with thick yellow smoke cloaking the works. In the 19th century, Redbrook became famous for its tin, the thinnest you could buy. The Redbrook Tinplate Company was famed around the world and in 1949 43,500 boxes of tinplate were produced weekly and exported worldwide, especially to the United States where it was used for packing tobacco.

THE WYE VALLEY WALK

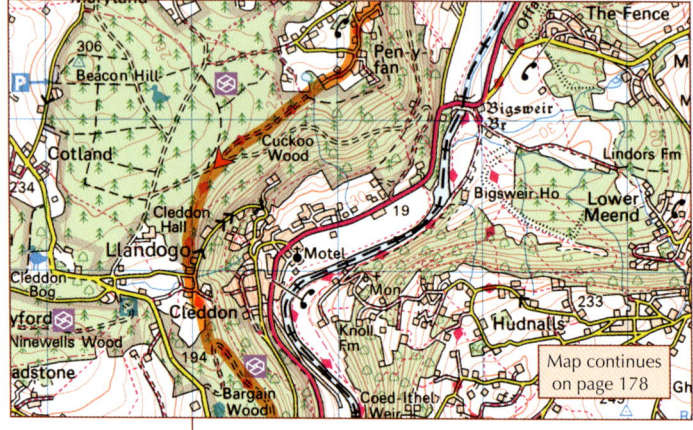

The Whitebrook, which cascades steeply down to the Wye, was harnessed to power wireworks in the 1600s and in 18th-century **paper mills**. By the 1790s six paper mills lined the Whitebrook making high grade paper for bank notes. The last mill closed in the 1880s but the ruins of the paper mills, the grand houses of the paper makers and the ponds which stored the water needed to power the waterwheels still line the banks of the Whitebrook.

Immediately after Whitebrook Farm, turn left up a steep and narrow path (lined with wild garlic in spring) between stone walls. At the junction of paths keep on climbing steeply uphill. After the steps at the top, turn left along the lane on another steep section past the Donkey Shed, then passing a beech wood full of snowdrops and bluebells in spring. The road curves uphill steeply to reach **Pen-y-fan Green**, a patch of open common land, where you can spot an old stone mounting block to the right, soon after the well-placed bench. ◀

Having just completed the climb you can understand why people remounted their horses and ponies here!

At the top of the Green, turn left after Spring Cottage along a grassy lane. After passing Horseshoe Barn, at the junction of paths turn right alongside a wooden garden fence and immediately right again up the path running between hedges. Turn left onto the road, keeping straight on at the junction to reach a gate where the tarmac ends and the path continues into woodland. Keep straight on along Duchess Ride.

This track, lined with Scots Pines, was the favourite ride of one of the duchesses of Beaufort and is now known as **Duchess Ride**. To admire the duchess's favourite view, look out for a narrow path to the left, which leads down to a conveniently placed bench where you can gaze out across the valley and spot the Severn Bridge.

Duchess Ride viewpoint to Brockweir (5.5km, 1hr 35min)

At the crossroads of tracks go straight ahead along a shaded path through mossy, boulder-strewn woodland. Ignore tracks off to either side to reach the hamlet of **Cleddon**. The route goes straight on passing Cleddon Falls to the left. If they are in full spate take the marked viewing route to the left to view the spectacle. Make sure you look up to see the multi-trunked beech tree (the result of coppicing) above you as you negotiate the handrail around its impressive roots and the slab of rock it appears to be growing out of. This is an outcrop of the 'puddingstone' used to make millstones

Cleddon Falls (photo: Michael Garland)

A RAINFOREST IN WALES

Cleddon Falls has long been a favourite with visitors. In the 19th century, construction of the Jubilee Walk created a refined way for Victorian sightseers and local people to scale the hillside. The path has recently been restored and leads down to Llandogo. This area is a Site of Special Scientific Interest. The waterfall cascading through this shady woodland creates the cool, humid conditions found in Celtic rainforests, perfect for moisture-loving lichens, mosses and liverworts which thrive here. Liverworts aren't usually found this far east but this is an unusually humid site which liverworts love. In the 1950s, the British Bryological Society sent their experts to survey the area, discovering a number of rare species which put Cleddon firmly on the map. Prickly featherwort and Hutchins' hollywort are just two of the highly unusual liverworts found here.

The waterfall is fed by the Cleddon Brook, which flows out of Cleddon Bog just under 1km away. Lowland peatlands such as Cleddon Bog are rare and this site was designated a Site of Special Scientific Interest 60 years ago. Cleddon Bog's flora includes bog asphodel, bog cottons, sphagnum mosses, cranberry and the carnivorous round-leaved sundew. As the bog's water levels have fallen, plants that like drier conditions such as purple moor grass and birch have become dominant, reducing the bog's ability to store water and carbon. Recently, hardy native-breed cattle have been introduced as part of a conservation grazing project. The cattle munch on the moor grass and trample the vegetation down, giving the sphagnum mosses and other bog plants a better chance of survival.

Keep straight on at the crossroads of paths soon after the waterfall, where a path to the left leads down to a historic viewpoint at the Bread and Cheese Stones.

Distinctive stone walls are a feature of this area. These two large stones are known locally as the **Bread and Cheese Stones**. This was a lookout for Cleddon residents, who would spot the trows coming up the river from Brockweir and race down to the quay to get work unloading cargo. William Wordsworth visited the Wye Valley twice and it is thought this view may have inspired his famous poem *Lines Composed a Few Miles Above Tintern Abbey*.

Continue up the walled track, ignoring the path to the right. Turn left along a wide track when you can see a bench and viewpoint. Follow this track down through **Bargain Wood** and around a forest barrier (passing a play area and **picnic benches** to the left) and continue downhill to another parking area at Whitestone. Just before the road turn left over a stream, to walk under tall pines. At the junction turn right down a narrow, eroded path, keeping left at the next fork. At the road go straight across and turn right through the wood to cross a stream. Later the path runs between giant redwoods and over a footbridge to meet the road at the entrance to the Botany Bay Activity Centre. Turn left, passing Hazel Grove, and immediately take the footpath to the left of the driveway to climb up through **Coed Beddick** woodland. Go straight ahead at the crossroads of tracks, continuing to climb. Stay on this track and turn left when you meet a wide track which descends through mature woodland. When the track forks keep left downhill to walk alongside the field boundary to your right, eventually reaching a gate and stile on your right. The route shown on your OS map may differ along this section down to Brockweir. (Self-catering cabin accommodation at the Wye Valley Sculpture Garden and the Hop Garden can be accessed by leaving the route and going through the gate on the right. A path leads down to the Wye Valley Sculpture Garden and the Hop Garden at Kingstone Brewery.)

Go straight ahead, passing a stone building on the right and going down steps to the left. Turn left at the bottom of steps. When the path forks take the left-hand fork past the electricity pole. Keep right as the path bears right around a tree, down steps and then straight on where the paths cross. At the junction turn right to walk down to the road. Cross the A466, turn right and immediately left, signposted **Brockweir**. (Leave the route here to reach Brockweir community shop and cafe by crossing the bridge and continuing uphill for 1km.)

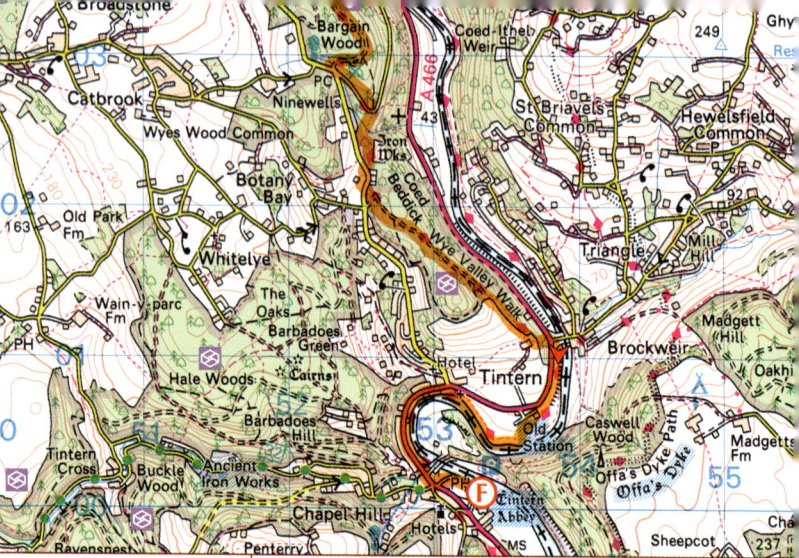

Brockweir to Tintern Abbey (2.7km, 45min)

Two hundred years ago, **Brockweir** was an important inland port. It was the main transfer point for the largest trows, which were assisted upriver by the tide. Here they unloaded their cargoes to lighter vessels for the trip above the tidal reach, with smaller boats serving Monmouth, Ross and Hereford. With at least 16 pubs, the village had a terrible reputation for the drunkenness and lawless character of the river men. In an attempt to save their souls a church was established in the village in 1832 by the Moravians, built on the site of the cock-fighting pit! It is still open today.

Straightaway, look out for steps on the right and take these steps down to the former railway line, which you follow to **Old Station Tintern**.

The Wye Valley Railway closed in 1964 making this **station** redundant until Monmouthshire County Council took over management of the site in the 1970s. Today there's a nostalgic feel to the place, with refurbished railway carriages displaying local history. The station booking office is now a (seasonal) cafe.

Walk past the old station and railway carriages, keeping left through the Circle of Legends sculptures on the line of the old railway track. Turn right down the steps, just before the river. Go through a gate and turn right to walk along the riverbank to Tintern. The path goes through the churchyard of **St Michael's Church**.

Circle of legends at the Old Station (photo: Cliff Spooner)

St Michael's Church was the site of an early Celtic church long before the Cistercian monks arrived to establish Tintern Abbey. In the 7th century King Tewdrig gave up his Kingdom of Gwent to live in Tintern as a hermit, but around AD630 invading Saxons attacked the local monasteries, prompting Tewdric to come out of retirement to defend the church. With his son, King Meurig, the Saxons were pushed back, but Tewdric was wounded and later died. **Tintern Parva** means 'little Tintern' in Latin and its thought the monks tended a vineyard here, where Parva Farm Vineyard is situated today, on the hillside above the church.

Approaching Tintern beside the now tidal Wye (photo: Gemma Kate Wood)

Leave the churchyard through an archway. Keep right and immediately turn left between the houses. At the A466 turn left to walk through Tintern. Cross the road at the bus stop and cross back at Abbey Mill to stay on the pavement. Abbey Mill is where the River Angidy flows into the Wye.

In spring and autumn, high tides can cause disruption along the route through Tintern. Any road closures are only for a short period of time around the highest point of the tide. See: www.tinternvillage.co.uk/public_services/tides.

THE ANGIDY VALLEY

Tintern has a rich industrial heritage. For 300 years Tintern's metal industries were at the cutting edge of industrial development in Britain and, by 1600, the largest industrial enterprise in Wales was located along the Angidy Valley. Abbey Mill was the focus of this activity as it was here, in a tidal dock, that raw materials were unloaded for the ironworks and forges located upstream on the Angidy, and finished iron products were loaded onto Wye trows for transport down the Wye. The remains of Abbey Furnace, a 17th-century ironworks, excavated and partially restored, can be viewed 1.7km up the Angidy Valley. Cannons were made at Abbey Furnace for use in the American War of Independence. (Download the Angidy Trail leaflet to find out more about the industrial heritage of this valley: www.wyevalley-nl.org.uk.)

STAGE 16 – MONMOUTH TO TINTERN

Opposite the Royal George turn left in front of the Filling Station Café to walk down the lane, bearing right in front of the old church and school room, passing Quay Cottage and continuing along the riverside to the Anchor Inn and **Tintern Abbey**, where this stage ends.

TINTERN

Tintern is a small village on the banks of the tidal Wye. With a long tradition of catering for the needs of travellers (first pilgrims to the abbey, later visitors on the Wye Tour), you will find a range of places to eat and drink (Anchor Inn, White Monk, Filling Station, the Hub ice cream shop, Rose & Crown, Royal George, Abbey Mill, Wye Valley Hotel, Parva Farmhouse, Old Station Tintern) as well as accommodation in two hotels, B&Bs and self-catering accommodation. There is a doctor's surgery, a small village shop, Kingstone Brewery, Parva Farm Vineyard and the Wye Valley Sculpture Garden, much loved for its snowdrops in February.

Tintern Abbey

This Gothic architectural masterpiece started life as a small timber building, founded in 1131 by the white-robed Cistercian monks. With the help of wealthy Marcher lords, construction of a new, stone abbey began in 1269, creating a magnificent structure with soaring arches and a seven-lancet window. Tintern became a victim of Henry VIII's destruction of the monasteries in 1536, when the lead roof tiles were removed and the abbey left to fall down, with locals helping themselves to building stone. Forgotten for 200 years, the Duke of Beaufort cleared the interior of overgrowth and rubble and from the 1760s the abbey became a must-see attraction for Wye Tourists, particularly after William Gilpin described Tintern Abbey as the 'most beautiful scene' of all on the Wye Tour. The abbey had become a victim of its own success by the 19th century, with steps, rails and planks installed so even elderly ladies could safely explore! Tourists complained of too many people spoiling the peace, picnicking and viewing the ruins at night by torchlight. In the 1880s, after the Wye Valley Railway opened, many more visitors arrived in their thousands to view the harvest moon rising through the abbey's rose window. Now a national icon, Tintern Abbey is cared for by Cadw, the Welsh government's historic environment service. *Cadw* is a Welsh word meaning 'to protect' or 'to keep'.

Tintern (photo: Gemma Kate Wood)

STAGE 17
Tintern to Chepstow

Start	Tintern Abbey SO 532 001
Finish	Chepstow Tourist Information Centre ST 532 942
Distance	9.6km (6 miles)
Time	3hr 45min
Ascent	470m (1540ft)
Terrain	Long climb to Black Cliff Wood, very short steep scramble; level path through woodland; descent to Lower Wyndcliff; some narrow sections with steep drops to side of path in Piercefield woods; roadside pavement in Chepstow
OS map	Explorer OL14 Wye Valley & Forest of Dean
Refreshments	None on route; hotels, pubs and cafés in Tintern and Chepstow
Public toilets	Tintern Abbey car park and adjacent to Chepstow Tourist Information Centre
Public transport	Bus service 69, hourly between Monmouth, Tintern and Chepstow

The final stage starts at Tintern Abbey, climbing out of the village to Black Cliff Wood. After a long woodland section one of the most expansive views on the Wye Valley Walk is revealed at the Eagle's Nest. Civilization seems closer as you near the end of the walk, but there's one last surprise after crossing the A466. The route follows paths laid out in the 18th century through the picturesque landscape of Piercefield Park, which was the highlight of the Wye Tour with its romantically named viewpoints and grotto. Passing through woodland, with steep drops down to the river, you emerge from the woods for the final section on roadside pavements and through Castle Dell in the shadow of Chepstow Castle, to the Tourist Information Centre. You will probably want to take a few more steps down to the Wye Bridge to say 'goodbye' to the river you have followed for the last 222km.

STAGE 17 – TINTERN TO CHEPSTOW

Tintern to the Eagle's Nest (3.5km, 1hr 30min)

From Tintern Abbey walk up to the A466 to cross the road in front of a post box and turn right up the lane. Hints of the ecclesiastical associations of this area can be seen in the arched gate. At St Anne's House bear left at the junction and walk behind the former Abbey Hotel. Cross the cattle grid, immediately turning left uphill along an ancient track. This is a garlic-lined path in springtime and soon passes limekilns on the right. The path climbs alongside a conifer plantation, and to the left you may be able to catch a glimpse of the river and abbey during winter months. The path becomes stony just before going through a gate where the view opens out across **Reddings Farm**. Bear right, to go through another gate and then head diagonally left across the field (the gateways in these fields can be extremely muddy when wet). Go through two more gates close together and head across this field to a gap in the hedge. Continue across the third field to the nearest corner of the wood in front of you. Catch your breath at the top, looking back at the view taking in the cottages dotted about on St Briavels Common. (Your OS map may show an old route for the Wye Valley Walk.)

Tintern Abbey (photo: Ed Moskalenko)

Go through the gate into Black Cliff Wood. Follow the track as it zigzags uphill, taking a sharp left turn towards the end of the climb where the path becomes very steep, with a few feet of clambering over stones, before reaching the top. The gnarled and weirdly shaped trees here give a mystical feel to this ancient wood. Follow the path to the left, which after a very short distance goes quickly down and up, where you can make out the ditch and banks of the **Black Cliff Iron Age hillfort**.

> The brooding presence of these massive **hillforts**, built by Iron Age tribes and commanding wide vistas high above the Wye, reinforces the feeling that this area has long been border country. Perhaps the Wye marked the border between the Dobunni and the Silures (the dominant Celtic tribe in south east Wales), or maybe the forts were designed to control the River Wye itself and its valuable trade.

You are now walking along the top of some of the highest river cliffs in Wales, with sheer drops to your left. Continue on this woodland path, ignoring tracks off to either side. Don't take the signed footpath to the left when you reach the field fence to your right, continue alongside the fence and then walk through a lovely copse of young beech trees. Look out for a gap in the trees to the left and a small Wye Valley Walk marker sign on the right, identifying a steep path leading down to the Eagle's Nest with its incredible view over the Lancaut peninsula, Chepstow Racecourse, Chepstow Castle and the Wye flowing out to meet its sister river the Severn. ◄ As you hear sounds of traffic below and see the River Severn in the distance, it's a sign that you are reaching the end of this magnificent walk. ◄

On a clear day you can see as far as North Devon.

*Download the Picturesque Piercefield leaflet to find out how this view is inextricably linked to sugar and slavery: **www.wyevalley-nl.org.uk**.*

> **The Eagle's Nest** is the first, or last (depending on which way you are walking), grand scene on the picturesque Piercefield walks, laid out in the 1750s by Valentine Morris, owner of the Piercefield estate. It was a double decker viewing platform perched on the edge of the cliff, but the lower deck has been removed

Stage 17 – Tintern to Chepstow

for safety. Look out for Victorian graffiti on the stonework. Piercefield, where the Wye makes two enormous bends, is one of the most outstanding examples of 18th-century picturesque landscape in Britain and is a Grade I registered historic park and garden. It became an unmissable attraction on the Wye Tour with Valentine's walks famed far and wide

The Eagle's Nest to Chepstow (6.1km, 2hr 15min)

Retrace your route up the steps and turn left. If you wish to take the extreme route down to the Lower Wyndcliff car park, follow the signs to the left for the Eagle's Nest Trail and the 365 Steps. These steps, one for each day of the year, were constructed by the Duke of Beaufort in 1828. They include a short, metal bridge with steps, and many narrow and often slippery stone steps, especially so in wet or humid weather. Alternatively, continue straight on downhill as the path descends gently to the Upper Wyndcliff car park. Turn left here to walk down through the wood. The junction of paths in the quarry marks where the 365 Steps route rejoins the main path.

> With the introduction of regular steam packet services from Bristol to Chepstow in the 1820s the number of visitors to Piercefield increased dramatically. Before long a romantic thatched cottage opened to provide refreshments for the travellers, located at the bottom of the 365 Steps. It was called **Moss Cottage** but sadly demolished in the 1950s.

The Wye Valley Walk now follows the paths designed by Valentine Morris all the way to Chepstow (sections can be very muddy in wet weather).

Turn right passing a forestry barrier to reach the **A466**. Cross the road and bear right to the far end of the Lower Wyndcliff car park where you will find the path continues. ◄ The path winds down through woodlands, with steep drops off to the left, eventually crossing a stream. This sheltered hollow was the site of the Cold Bath.

> The remains of the **Cold Bath** in the undergrowth include a plunge pool, where a few white ceramic tiles remain on the walls, and what is thought to have been the dressing room, which is now a pile of rubble.

Keep on the path, which becomes narrow and windy with steep drops to the side down to the river, stones and exposed tree roots, bounded by beautiful ferns glowing green in the dappled light. Eventually the path starts to rise and in the distance you can make out the dark stone entrance to the Giant's Cave. Walk through to the spectacular view which greets you on the other side.

> The **Giant's Cave** is one of the most dramatic features on the Piercefield walk, with a viewing platform built into the rock face by the entrance to the cave. The cave is not natural but was hewn out of

STAGE 17 – TINTERN TO CHEPSTOW

the rock. Engineered to surprise, it was all part of the Piercefield experience. A visitor in 1781 advised to, 'Carry some gunpowder and leave it with Mr Morris's gardener in order to fire some small cannon on the Rock as you pass by. The reverberating echo of which you will find has a wonderful effect.' At one time a stone giant stood above the cave entrance, holding a huge boulder over his head, as if about to hurl it on the walkers below. Sadly the giant, and his boulder, suffered from frost damage and slowly crumbled away.

At the junction of paths carry straight on, winding around the cliff face and the exposed roots of ancient yew trees, with steep drops to the left. Further along pass a giant stone in the middle of the path, which was one of a circle of upright stones known as the Druid's Temple. Shortly after is a yellow waymarker post indicating a path on the right.

If you would like to view **Piercefield House**, where Valentine Morris lived, turn right here to take a very short detour over a stile. The ruined mansion is on the right, with expansive views to the left and Chepstow Racecourse straight ahead.

The Eagle's Nest at the start of the Piercefield walks (photo: Gemma Kate Wood)

ANCIENT WOODLAND

The Lower Wye Valley woodlands are one of largest and most important areas of native woodland remaining in Britain. Piercefield woods contain whitebeam species that are only found here, and it is the only place in Wales where the Cosnard's net-winged beetle is found. Piercefield also has many very old yew trees and as a result these woods are protected as a Special Area of Conservation.

The Wye Valley Walk keeps straight on and the path becomes less precipitous, passing what was the Double View, where once you could see the Severn to the right and the Wye to the left. Opening out to a more cleared area you soon pass the remains of the Grotto on the right.

> It was the height of fashion to have a **grotto**. This one was lined with quartz crystals, iron cinders and copper – you may spot a few surviving pieces. Two hundred years ago this was a spectacular view of grand distances, taking in much of Gloucestershire beyond the Severn.

The path turns sharp right after a short downhill section of tree roots and steps and then bears to the left (ignore track to right). Follow steps down, passing giant horse chestnut and beech trees probably planted in the 1750s by Valentine Morris and now veteran trees. Follow the path to the left again until reaching some yew trees and, on the left, metal railings, which mark the site of the Platform, another (now lost) viewpoint.

> At one time you could see Chepstow Castle and the Lancaut cliffs from the **Platform**, but today these woods are internationally important for their nature conservation value. The viewing platform is a romantic remnant of a past landscape when the view was more highly prized.

Ignore the path to the right when you can see railings in the distance. Follow the railings round to the left

Stage 17 – Tintern to Chepstow

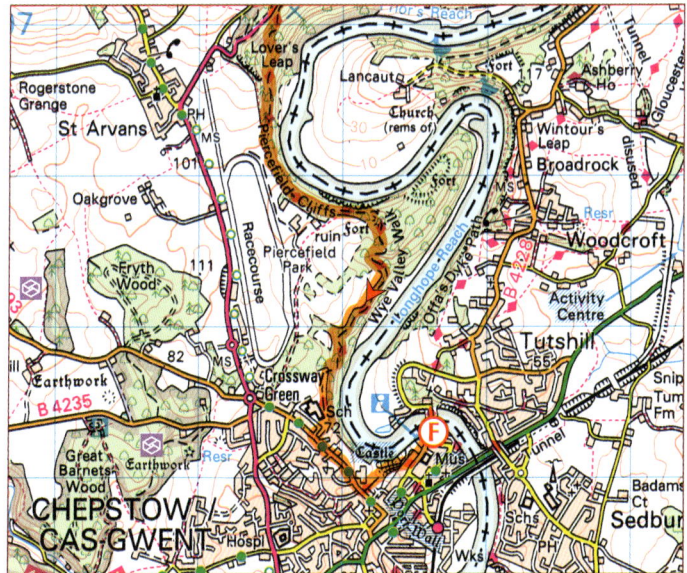

to the final viewpoint, the Alcove, which looks towards Chepstow Castle.

> The **Alcove** was the first of the viewpoints, constructed around 1750. A small building with an arched opening stood here, framing the view of the town and castle.

Follow the path from the Alcove up a flight of steps and left through a gap in the stone wall. Continue along a fenced path which emerges beside the Wye Valley Walk sculptural marker in Chepstow Leisure Centre car park. Walk slightly to the left to leave the car park, turning left onto the main road and following the pavement downhill. Soon after passing The Dell Primary School turn left onto the footpath through the Castle Dell, walking beside the imposing fortifications of **Chepstow Castle**. The large stone boulder on the right, just before the car park, marks

THE WYE VALLEY WALK

This sculptural waymarker greets you as you arrive in Chepstow

the official end (or start) of the Wye Valley Walk. Cross the car park to Chepstow Tourist Information Centre to collect your last passport stamp and, if you wish to pay a final farewell to the river that has been your companion for the last 222km, turn left at the information centre and walk down to the Wye Bridge and riverside area. From here you can continue walking on Offa's Dyke National Trail and the Wales Coast Path!

CHEPSTOW

Chepstow has all the facilities and services you may need with a good selection of places to eat, drink and stay and some interesting independent shops along pedestrianised St Mary's Street. Adjacent to the medieval castle is the Tourist Information Centre and Chepstow Museum, which has an impressive collection of paintings, prints, sketches and diaries by Wye Tourists (some famous, many unknown) providing a tantalising glimpse of the landscape of the Wye over the past 250 years. A stroll along the riverfront area will take you to where tourists arrived and departed in the 19th century on the steam packet boats from Bristol. Further along near the railway bridge you can find the *Severn Princess*, the last survivor of the ferry boats that connected South Wales to England before the Severn Bridges were built. Today trains run between Gloucester, Severn Tunnel Junction (for Bristol), Newport and Cardiff and National Express buses for London and Cardiff stop here.

Chepstow Castle

Perched on limestone cliffs high above the Wye, Chepstow Castle is the first stone-built Norman castle in Britain. Started in 1067 the castle evolved over the following 600 years to deal with newer destructive weapons. Even the castle doors were sheathed in iron to stop attacks and flaming arrows. They are the oldest castle doors in Europe, dating from the 1190s, and now safely displayed in the castle's gatehouse. It is now cared for by Cadw, who protect historic buildings in Wales.

The port of Chepstow

During the mediaeval period Chepstow became the largest port in Wales because it had an advantage over other ports. It was exempt from English taxation as it was controlled by the Marcher lords and not the king. Large ships carrying imports could be brought into the deep water of the Wye at Chepstow and then transferred to the smaller Wye trows for journeys many miles inland. Sea faring vessels voyaged to France and Portugal, as the import of wine was particularly significant. The port flourished and between 1790 and 1795 Chepstow handled more goods than Cardiff, Newport and Swansea. Exports included timber for ship building and bark for use in the tanning industry, and wire and paper manufactured in Tintern, Redbrook and Whitebrook. Chepstow remained the most important port in South Wales until the 19th century when the export of coal and iron saw Cardiff, Newport and Swansea, nearer the coalfield, take over Chepstow's long held position.

Journey's end at Chepstow's clifftop castle

APPENDIX A
Tourist information and useful contacts

Tourist information centres

Hay-on-Wye Tourist Information Centre
Chapel Cottage
Oxford Road
Hay-on-Wye
HR3 5DG
tel 01497 820144
post@hay-on-wye.co.uk

Hereford Tourist Information Centre
Town Hall
St Owen's St
Hereford
HR1 2PJ
tel 01432 383837
tic@herefordcitycouncil.gov.uk

Ross-on-Wye Tourist Information Outlet
Made in Ross
Market House
Ross-on-Wye
tel 01989 562373
tourism@rosstc-herefordshire.gov.uk

Monmouth Tourist Information Outlet
Shire Hall
Agincourt Square
Monmouth
NP25 3DY
tel 01600 775257
shirehall@monmouthshire.gov.uk

Chepstow Tourist Information Centre
Castle Car Park
Bridge Street
Chepstow
NP16 5EY
tel 01291 623772
chepstow.tic@monmouthshire.gov.uk

Tourism websites

Wye Valley Walk
www.wyevalleywalk.org

Wye Valley National Landscape
www.wyevalley-nl.org.uk

Visit Wales
www.visitwales.com

Mid Wales
www.midwalesmyway.com

Visit Cambrian Mountains
www.thecambrianmountains.co.uk

Visit Herefordshire
www.visitherefordshire.co.uk

Visit Monmouthshire
www.visitmonmouthshire.com

Wye Valley & Forest of Dean Tourism
www.visitdeanwye.co.uk

Appendix A – Tourist information and useful contacts

Travel information

Trains
National Rail enquiries
tel 03457 48 49 50
www.nationalrail.co.uk

Transport for Wales
tel 03333 211 202
https://tfw.wales

Coach and bus
Traveline Cymru
tel 08004 640 000
www.traveline.cymru

Traveline England
www.traveline.info

National Express (coaches)
www.nationalexpress.com/en

Bus timetables in Powys
https://en.powys.gov.uk/bustimetables

Bus services in Herefordshire
www.herefordshire.gov.uk/public-transport-1/bus-travel

Bus and coach information
https://bustimes.org
This is a useful site in that you can type in the name of a place and it will come up with a list of services running through the town and furnish you with timetables for each route.

APPENDIX B
Walking holiday companies and baggage transfer

Holiday companies

Celtic Trails
tel 01291 689774
www.celtictrailswalkingholidays.co.uk

Contours Walking Holidays
tel 01629 821900
www.contours.co.uk

Drover Holidays
tel 01497 821134
www.droverholidays.co.uk

Embark Walking Holidays
tel 01873 379100
www.embarkwalkingholidays.com

Let's go Walking
tel 01837 880075
www.letsgowalking.co.uk

Ramblers Walking Holidays
tel 01707 537507
www.ramblersholidays.co.uk

Wales Walking Holidays
tel 07483 229606
https://waleswalkingholidays.com/wye-valley-walk

Baggage transfer

WALKLite
(Hay-on-Wye to Chepstow)
tel 07852 282319
info@walklitebt.co.uk
https://walklitebt.co.uk

Eco Carriers Luggage Transfer
(within 20 miles of Kington including sections of the Wye Valley Walk)
tel 01544 327 758
geoffandpatsy@kayoss.co.uk

Kenny's Taxis
(Glasbury to Chepstow)
tel 07828 882432
www.kennystaxis.com

Hay taxibus luggage transfers
(between Builth, Hay-on-Wye, Bredwardine and Hereford)
tel 01497820444 or 07974106656
https://haytaxibus.co.uk/luggage-transfers

Woods Taxis
(Between Hay-on-Wye, Builth Wells, Rhayader and Llangurig)
01982 552709 or 07917 663363
https://woodstaxi.com

Sprigg's Taxis, Rhayader
(Between Rhayader, Llangurig and Llanidloes)
07368 496089

Tour guides

Wales official tourist guides
www.walesbestguides.com

APPENDIX C
Where to collect your passport stamps

Stage		Stamp location
At the start	Rhyd-y-benwch carpark	On 'All Walks' start sign
Stage 1	Rhyd-y-benwch to Llangurig	Llangurig Post Office and Stores
Stage 2	Llangurig to Rhayader	CARAD Museum, East Street, Rhayader
Stage 3	Rhayader to Newbridge	Newbridge Post Office
Stage 4	Newbridge to Builth Wells	Bronwye B&B, Church St, Builth Wells
Stage 5	Builth Wells to Erwood	Erwood Station Craft Centre (on glass window on left of entrance door)
Stage 6	Erwood to Glasbury	Paddler's Rest Cafe at the River Wye Activity Centre, Glasbury
Stage 7	Glasbury to Hay-on-Wye	W Golesworthy & Sons, Broad St, Hay-on-Wye
Stage 8	Hay-on-Wye to Bredwardine	St Andrew's Church, Bredwardine/Red Lion Hotel, Bredwardine
Stage 9	Bredwardine to Byford	St John's Church, Byford
Stage 10	Byford to Hereford	Hereford Tourist Information Centre, Town Hall, St Owen's Street
Stage 11	Hereford to Fownhope	St Mary's Church, Fownhope
Stage 12	Fownhope to Ross-on-Wye	Hope & Anchor, Ross-on-Wye Riverside
Stage 13	Ross-on-Wye to Kerne Bridge	Inn on the Wye at Kerne Bridge
Stage 14	Kerne Bridge to Symonds Yat	Saracen's Head Inn, Symonds Yat East
Stage 15	Symonds Yat to Monmouth	Stephen's Book Shop, Church Street, Monmouth
Stage 16	Monmouth to Tintern	Old Station, Tintern
Stage 17	Tintern to Chepstow	Chepstow Tourist Information Centre, Bridge Street

APPENDIX D
Reporting a problem on a right of way

Powys route sections
These route sections are in Powys and maintained by Powys County Council:

- Stage 1 Rhyd-y-Benwch to Llangurig
- Stage 2 Llangurig to Rhayader
- Stage 3 Rhayader to Newbridge
- Stage 4 Newbridge to Builth Wells
- Stage 5 Builth Wells to Erwood
- Stage 6 Erwood to Glasbury
- Stage 7 Glasbury to Hay-on-Wye

Report a problem in Powys:
https://en.powys.gov.uk/article/2589/Report-a-concern-with-a-right-of-way

Herefordshire route sections
These route sections are maintained by Herefordshire Council:

- Stage 8 Hay to Bredwardine
- Stage 9 Bredwardine to Byford
- Stage 10 Byford to Hereford
- Stage 11 Hereford to Fownhope
- Stage 12 Fownhope to Ross-on-Wye
- Stage 13 Ross-on-Wye to Kerne Bridge

Report a problem in Herefordshire:
www.herefordshire.gov.uk/public-rights-way

Herefordshire and Gloucestershire route sections
This section is partly in Herefordshire and partly in Gloucestershire:

- Stage 14 Kerne Bridge to Symonds Yat

Report a problem in Herefordshire:
www.herefordshire.gov.uk/public-rights-way
Report a problem in Gloucestershire:
https://fixmystreet.gloucestershire.gov.uk/

Gloucestershire and Monmouthshire route sections
This section is partly in Gloucestershire and partly in Monmouthshire:

- Stage 15 Symonds Yat to Monmouth

Report a problem in Gloucestershire:
https://fixmystreet.gloucestershire.gov.uk/
Report a problem in Monmouthshire:
www.herefordshire.gov.uk/public-rights-way

Monmouthshire route sections
These sections are in Monmouthshire:

- Stage 16 Monmouth to Tintern
- Stage 17 Tintern to Chepstow

Report a problem in Monmouthshire:
https://access.monmouthshire.gov.uk

APPENDIX E
Further reading

Andrew Allott, *Marches* (Collins New Naturalist Library, 2011)

John Berger and Jean Mohr, *A Fortunate Man* (Canongate Canons, 2016)

Francis Kilvert, *Kilvert's Diary 1870–1879* (Jonathan Cape, 1944)

George Peterkin, *Wye Valley* (Collins New Naturalists Library, 2008)

George Peterkin, Tim Crave and Christiana Payne, *Art Meets Ecology: The Arborealists in Lady Park Wood* (Sansom & Co, 2020)

Julian Mitchell, *The Wye Tour* (Logaston Press, 2010)

Polly Morland, *A Fortunate Woman* (Picador, 2022); the best-selling follow up to *A Fortunate Man*

Robert Gibbings, *Coming down the Wye* (JM Dent & Sons, 1942)

Steve Clarke, *The Lost Lake* (Clarke Printing, 2013)

William Gilpin, *Observations on the River Wye* (Pallas Athene, 2005)

Wye Valley AONB, *Overlooking the Wye* (Black Dwarf Publications, 2013)

Matthew Hall's series of novels about Jenny Cooper, the Bristol-based coroner who lives in the Wye Valley, offers rip-roaring reads by an author who also lives in the Wye Valley.

APPENDIX F
Selected accommodation options

Check out www.wyevalleywalk.org/walk for a map showing the location of accommodation all along the route.

Stage 1 Rhyd-y-benwch to Llangurig
Glangwy Farm Camping
https://glangwyfarm.com

Plas Bwlch B&B
www.bandbwales.co.uk

The Old Vicarage
www.theoldvicaragellangurig.co.uk

The Bluebell Inn
www.bluebell-inn.co.uk

Stage 2 Llangurig to Rhayader
The Clochfaen B&B
www.theclochfaen.com

Coed Cochion Glamping Domes
www.redwoodretreat.co.uk

Wyeside Camping
www.campingandcaravanningclub.co.uk

Bryn Derwyn B&B
www.brynderwenbedandbreakfast.co.uk

Ty Morgans
www.croesogrwp.com/accommodation-ty-morgans

The Crown
https://www.croesogrwp.com/the-crown-inn-rhayader

The Elan Hotel
www.elanhotelrhayader.co.uk

Stage 3 Rhayader to Newbridge
Doliago Farm Camping
https://doliago.com

Vulcan Lodge Cottages
www.littlewelshgetaways.co.uk

Disserth Camping
https://disserth.biz/info/location

Stage 4 Newbridge to Builth Wells
Pwllgwylim B&B
www.pwllgwilym-bandb.co.uk

Bron Wye Guest House
www.facebook.com/BronwyeGuestHouse

The Owls B&B
https://theowlsbuilthwells.co.uk

Celtic Woodland Holidays Camping Pods
www.celticwoodlandholidays.co.uk

Cae Berris Manor
https://caerberis.com

Stage 5 Builth Wells to Erwood
Pwll-y-faedda B&B
https://pwll-y-faedda.co.uk

The Skreen
https://theskreen.uk

Great House Farm Glamping
https://greathousefarm.co.uk

The Pantry B&B
www.thepantrybandb.co.uk

Stage 6 Erwood to Glasbury
Llangoed Hall Hotel
www.llangoedhall.co.uk

Appendix F – Selected accommodation options

Griffin Inn
https://thegriffinllyswen.com

Cwmbach Lodge
https://cwmbachlodge.co.uk

Glasbury B&B
https://www.glasburybnb.co.uk

Foyles
https://foylesofglasbury.co.uk

Aberllynfi Riverside House
www.aberllynfi.house

Stage 7 Glasbury to Hay-on-Wye
Seren Bach Campsite
www.haycamping.com

Racquety Farm
www.racquetyfarm.com

The Swan at Hay
www.swanathay.co.uk

The Seven Stars B&B
www.theseven-stars.co.uk

The Firs
www.thefirsathay.com

Kilverts
https://kilverts.co.uk

The Old Black Lion
www.oldblacklion.co.uk

Stage 8 Hay-on-Wye to Bredwardine
Drovers Rest
www.droversrest.co.uk

The Smithy B&B
https://thesmithybedandbreakfast.com

Heart of the Wye Glamping
www.heartofthewye.co.uk

Locksters Pool Camping
www.campingriverwye.co.uk

Whitney Bridge Glamping
www.whitneybridge.com

The Boat Inn
www.boatinn-whitney.co.uk

Agent's House B&B
www.whitneyonwyebandb.co.uk

The Red Lion Hotel
www.redlion-hotel.com

Stage 9 Bredwardine to Byford
Dairy House Farm B&B
www.dairyhousefarm.org

Maggie's Field Camping
www.maggiesfield.camp

Byford Glamping
www.byfordglamping.co.uk

Stage 10 Byford to Hereford
The Priory Hotel
https://theprioryhereford.co.uk

Hereford Rowing Club Campsite
www.herefordrc.co.uk/campsite

Castle House Hotel
https://castlehse.co.uk

The Green Dragon Hotel
www.greendragonhotel.com

Charades Guest House
www.charadeshereford.co.uk

The Green Man
www.thegreenman.co

The Bowens B&B
www.bowensbandb.co.uk

Stage 12 Fownhope to Ross-on-Wye
Caplor Glamping & Lodges
www.caplorglamping.com

The Falcon House
https://thefalconhouse.co.uk

White House Glamping
https://whitehouseonwye.co.uk

The Wye Valley Walk

Mad dogs and vintage vans
https://maddogsandvintagevans.co.uk

White Lion Camping
www.whitelionross.com/camping

The Radcliffe Guesthouse
https://radcliffeguesthouse.co.uk

The Bridge House
www.bridgehouserossonwye.co.uk

Orles Barn B&B
www.orlesbarn.co.uk

Benhall Farm B&B
https://benhallfarm.co.uk

Broom Farm Orchard Camping
https://rosscider.com

Broom Farm Guesthouse
https://broomefarmhouse.co.uk

The Hope and Anchor
www.thehopeandanchor.co.uk

The White House Guesthouse
www.whitehouseross.com

King's Head Hotel
https://kingshead.co.uk

Bridgstow Guesthouse
www.bridstowguesthouse.co.uk

Stage 13 Ross-on-Wye to Kerne Bridge
Lower Wythall B&B
www.lowerwythall.co.uk

Wythall Estate
https://wythallestate.co.uk

Inn on the Wye
www.innonthewye.co.uk

The Hostelrie
https://thehostelrieatgoodrich.co.uk

Stage 14 Kerne Bridge to Symonds Yat
YHA Wye Valley
www.yha.org.uk

Saracens Head
www.saracensheadinn.co.uk

Royal Hotel
https://royalhotel-symondsyat.com

Ye Olde Ferrie Inn
www.yeoldferrieinn.com

Old Court Hotel
https://oldcourthotel.co.uk

Paddocks Hotel
www.paddockshotel.com

Stage 15 Symonds Yat to Monmouth
Biblins Youth Campsite
www.biblinsyouthcampsite.org

Creates B&B
www.createsmonmouth.com/bandb

The Punch House
https://thepunchhousemonmouth.co.uk

Premier Inn Monmouth
www.premierinn.com

The Riverside Hotel
www.riversidehotelmonmouth.co.uk

Stage 16 Monmouth to Tintern
The Mayhill Hotel
http://themayhillhotel.com

Inglewood Guesthouse
https://inglewoodhousewyevalley.co.uk

The Whitebrook
www.thewhitebrook.co.uk

Highlands Holidays
https://highlandsholidaysmonmouth.com

Parva Farmhouse
www.parvafarmhouse.co.uk

The Wye Valley Hotel
www.thewyevalleyhotel.co.uk

Appendix F – Selected accommodation options

Stage 17 Tintern to Chepstow
Fairoaks Lakes pods
www.pitchup.com

Woodfield House
www.woodfield.house

The First Hurdle
https://thefirsthurdle.co.uk

Two Rivers Hotel Chepstow
www.marstonsinns.co.uk/inns

Coach & Horses
www.coachchepstow.co.uk

Beaufort Hotel
www.beauforthotelchepstow.com

No 8
www.booking.com

The Three Tuns
http://the-three-tuns.hotels-wales.com

DOWNLOAD THE ROUTES IN GPX FORMAT

All the routes in this guide are available for download from:

www.cicerone.co.uk/1198/gpx

as standard format GPX files. You should be able to load them into most online GPX systems and mobile devices, whether GPS or smartphone. You may need to convert the file into your preferred format using a conversion programme such as gpsvisualizer.com or one of the many other such websites and programmes.

When you follow this link, you will be asked for your email address and where you purchased the guidebook, and have the option to subscribe to the Cicerone e-newsletter.

www.cicerone.co.uk

LISTING OF CICERONE GUIDES

BRITISH ISLES CHALLENGES, COLLECTIONS AND ACTIVITIES
Great Walks on the England Coast Path
Map and Compass
The Big Rounds
The Book of the Bivvy
The Book of the Bothy
The Mountains of England and Wales:
 Vol 1 Wales
 Vol 2 England
The National Trails
Walking the End to End Trail

SHORT WALKS SERIES
Short Walks Hadrian's Wall
Short Walks in the Lake District: Keswick, Borrowdale and Buttermere
Short Walks in the Lake District: Windermere Ambleside and Grasmere
Short Walks in the Lake District: Coniston and Langdale
Short Walks in Arnside and Silverdale
Short Walks in Nidderdale
Short Walks in Northumberland: Wooler, Rothbury, Alnwick and the coast
Short Walks on the Malvern Hills
Short Walks in Cornwall: Falmouth and the Lizard
Short Walks in Cornwall: Land's End and Penzance
Short Walks in the South Downs: Brighton, Eastbourne and Arundel
Short Walks in the Surrey Hills
Short Walks Winchester
Short Walks in Pembrokeshire: Tenby and the south
Short Walks on the Isle of Mull
Short Walks on the Orkney Islands

SCOTLAND
Ben Nevis and Glen Coe
Cycling in the Hebrides
Cycling the North Coast 500
Great Mountain Days in Scotland
Mountain Biking in Southern and Central Scotland
Mountain Biking in West and North West Scotland
Not the West Highland Way Scotland
Scotland's Best Small Mountains
Scotland's Mountain Ridges
Scottish Wild Country Backpacking
Short Walks in Dumfries and Galloway
Skye's Cuillin Ridge Traverse
The Borders Abbeys Way
The Great Glen Way
The Great Glen Way Map Booklet
The Hebridean Way
The Hebrides
The Isle of Mull
The Isle of Skye
The Skye Trail
The Southern Upland Way
The West Highland Way
West Highland Way Map Booklet
Walking Ben Lawers, Rannoch and Atholl
Walking in the Cairngorms
Walking in the Pentland Hills
Walking in the Scottish Borders
Walking in the Southern Uplands
Walking in Torridon, Fisherfield, Fannichs and An Teallach
Walking Loch Lomond and the Trossachs
Walking on Arran
Walking on Harris and Lewis
Walking on Jura, Islay and Colonsay
Walking on Rum and the Small Isles
Walking on the Orkney and Shetland Isles
Walking on Uist and Barra
Walking the Cape Wrath Trail
Walking the Corbetts
 Vol 1 South of the Great Glen
 Vol 2 North of the Great Glen
Walking the Galloway Hills
Walking the John o' Groats Trail
Walking the Munros
 Vol 1 — Southern, Central and Western Highlands
 Vol 2 — Northern Highlands and the Cairngorms
Winter Climbs in the Cairngorms
Winter Climbs: Ben Nevis and Glen Coe

NORTHERN ENGLAND ROUTES
Cycling the Reivers Route
Cycling the Way of the Roses
Hadrian's Cycleway
Hadrian's Wall Path
Hadrian's Wall Path Map Booklet
Pennine Way Map Booklet
The Coast to Coast Cycle Route
The Coast to Coast Walk
The Coast to Coast Map Booklet
The Pennine Way
Walking the Dales Way
The Dales Way Map Booklet

LAKE DISTRICT
Bikepacking in the Lake District
Cycling in the Lake District
Great Mountain Days in the Lake District
Joss Naylor's Lakes, Meres and Waters of the Lake District
Lake District Winter Climbs
Lake District:
 High Level and Fell Walks
 Low Level and Lake Walks
Mountain Biking in the Lake District
Outdoor Adventures with Children — Lake District
Scrambles in the Lake District —
 North
 South
Trail and Fell Running in the Lake District
Walking The Cumbria Way
Walking the Lake District Fells —
 Borrowdale
 Buttermere
 Coniston
 Keswick
 Langdale
 Mardale and the Far East
 Patterdale
 Wasdale
Walking the Tour of the Lake District

NORTH—WEST ENGLAND AND THE ISLE OF MAN
Cycling the Pennine Bridleway
Isle of Man Coastal Path
The Lancashire Cycleway
The Lune Valley and Howgills
Walking in Cumbria's Eden Valley
Walking in Lancashire
Walking in the Forest of Bowland and Pendle
Walking on the Isle of Man
Walking on the West Pennine Moors
Walking the Ribble Way
Walks in Silverdale and Arnside

NORTH—EAST ENGLAND, YORKSHIRE DALES AND PENNINES
Cycling in the Yorkshire Dales
Great Mountain Days in the Pennines
Mountain Biking in the Yorkshire Dales
The Cleveland Way and the Yorkshire Wolds Way
The Cleveland Way Map Booklet
The North York Moors
Trail and Fell Running in the Yorkshire Dales
Walking in County Durham
Walking in Northumberland
Walking in the North Pennines
Walking in the Yorkshire Dales:
 North and East
 South and West
Walking St Cuthbert's Way
Walking St Oswald's Way and Northumberland Coast Path

DERBYSHIRE, PEAK DISTRICT AND MIDLANDS
Cycling in the Peak District
Dark Peak Walks
Scrambles in the Dark Peak
Walking in Derbyshire
Walking in the Peak District — White Peak East
Walking in the Peak District — White Peak West

WALES AND WELSH BORDERS
Cycle Touring in Wales
Cycling Lon Las Cymru
Great Mountain Days in Snowdonia
Hillwalking in Shropshire
Mountain Walking in Snowdonia
Offa's Dyke Path
Offa's Dyke Map Booklet
Scrambles in Snowdonia
Snowdonia: 30 Low-level and Easy Walks
— North
— South
The Cambrian Way
The Pembrokeshire Coast Path
Pembrokeshire Coast Path Map Booklet
The Snowdonia Way
The Wye Valley Walk
Walking Glyndwr's Way
Walking in Carmarthenshire
Walking in Pembrokeshire
Walking in the Brecon Beacons
Walking in the Forest of Dean
Walking in the Wye Valley
Walking on Gower
Walking the Severn Way
Walking the Shropshire Way
Walking the Wales Coast Path

SOUTHERN ENGLAND
20 Classic Sportive Rides in South East England
20 Classic Sportive Rides in South West England
Cycling in the Cotswolds
Mountain Biking on the North Downs
Mountain Biking on the South Downs
Suffolk Coast and Heath Walks
The Cotswold Way
The Cotswold Way Map Booklet
The Kennet and Avon Canal
The Lea Valley Walk
The North Downs Way
North Downs Way Map Booklet
The Peddars Way and Norfolk Coast Path
The Pilgrims' Way
The Ridgeway National Trail
The Ridgeway Map Booklet
The South Downs Way
The South Downs Way Map Booklet
The Thames Path
The Thames Path Map Booklet
The Two Moors Way
Two Moors Way Map Booklet
Walking Hampshire's Test Way
Walking in Cornwall
Walking in Essex
Walking in Kent
Walking in London
Walking in Norfolk
Walking in the Chilterns
Walking in the Cotswolds
Walking in the Isles of Scilly
Walking in the New Forest
Walking in the North Wessex Downs
Walking on Dartmoor
Walking on Guernsey
Walking on Jersey
Walking on the Isle of Wight
Walking the Dartmoor Way
Walking the Jurassic Coast
Walking the Sarsen Way
Walking the South West Coast Path
South West Coast Path Map Booklet
— Vol 1: Minehead to St Ives
— Vol 2: St Ives to Plymouth
— Vol 3: Plymouth to Poole
Walks in the South Downs National Park
Cycling Land's End to John o' Groats

ALPS CROSS—BORDER ROUTES
100 Hut Walks in the Alps
Alpine Ski Mountaineering Vol 1 — Western Alps
The Karnischer Hohenweg
The Tour of the Bernina
Trail Running — Chamonix and the Mont Blanc region
Trekking Chamonix to Zermatt
Trekking in the Alps
Trekking in the Silvretta and Ratikon Alps
Trekking Munich to Venice
Trekking the Tour du Mont Blanc
Tour du Mont Blanc Map Booklet
Walking in the Alps

FRANCE, BELGIUM, AND LUXEMBOURG
Camino de Santiago — Via Podiensis
Chamonix Mountain Adventures
Cycle Touring in France
Cycling London to Paris
Cycling the Canal de la Garonne
Cycling the Canal du Midi
Mont Blanc Walks
Mountain Adventures in the Maurienne
Short Treks on Corsica
The GR5 Trail
The GR5 Trail — Vosges and Jura Benelux and Lorraine
The Grand Traverse of the Massif Central
The Moselle Cycle Route
Trekking in the Vanoise
Trekking the Cathar Way
Trekking the GR10
Trekking the GR20 Corsica
Trekking the Robert Louis Stevenson Trail
Via Ferratas of the French Alps
Walking in Provence — East
Walking in Provence — West
Walking in the Auvergne
Walking in the Brianconnais
Walking in the Dordogne
Walking in the Haute Savoie: North
Walking in the Haute Savoie: South
Walking on Corsica
Walking the Brittany Coast Path
Walking in the Ardennes

PYRENEES AND FRANCE/SPAIN CROSS—BORDER ROUTES
Shorter Treks in the Pyrenees
The Pyrenean Haute Route
The Pyrenees
Trekking the Cami dels Bons Homes
Trekking the GR11 Trail
Walks and Climbs in the Pyrenees

SPAIN AND PORTUGAL
Camino de Santiago: Camino Frances
Costa Blanca Mountain Adventures
Cycling the Camino de Santiago
Mountain Walking in Mallorca
Mountain Walking in Southern Catalunya
Spain's Sendero Historico: The GR1
The Andalucian Coast to Coast Walk
The Camino del Norte and Camino Primitivo
The Camino Ingles and Ruta do Mar
The Mountains Around Nerja
The Sierras of Extremadura
Trekking in Mallorca
Trekking in the Canary Islands
Trekking the GR7 in Andalucia
Walking and Trekking in the Sierra Nevada
Walking in Andalucia
Walking in Catalunya — Barcelona
Girona Pyrenees
Walking in the Picos de Europa
Walking La Via de la Plata and Camino Sanabres
Walking on Gran Canaria
Walking on La Gomera and El Hierro
Walking on La Palma
Walking on Lanzarote and Fuerteventura
Walking on Tenerife
Walking on the Costa Blanca
Walking the Camino dos Faros
Portugal's Rota Vicentina
The Camino Portugues
Walking in Portugal
Walking in the Algarve

Walking on Madeira
Walking on the Azores

SWITZERLAND
Switzerland's Jura Crest Trail
The Swiss Alps
Tour of the Jungfrau Region
Trekking the Swiss Via Alpina
Walking in Arolla and Zinal
Walking in the Bernese Oberland — Jungfrau region
Walking in the Engadine — Switzerland
Walking in the Valais
Walking in Ticino
Walking in Zermatt and Saas—Fee

GERMANY
Hiking and Cycling in the Black Forest
The Danube Cycleway Vol 1
The Rhine Cycle Route
The Westweg
Walking in the Bavarian Alps

POLAND, SLOVAKIA, ROMANIA, HUNGARY AND BULGARIA
The Danube Cycleway Vol 2
The High Tatras
The Mountains of Romania

SCANDINAVIA, ICELAND AND GREENLAND
Hiking in Norway — South
Trekking the Kungsleden
Trekking in Greenland — The Arctic Circle Trail
Walking and Trekking in Iceland

SLOVENIA, CROATIA, SERBIA, MONTENEGRO AND ALBANIA
Hiking Slovenia's Juliana Trail
Mountain Biking in Slovenia
The Islands of Croatia
The Julian Alps of Slovenia
The Mountains of Montenegro
The Peaks of the Balkans Trail
The Slovene Mountain Trail
Walking in Slovenia: The Karavanke
Walks and Treks in Croatia

ITALY
Alta Via 1 — Trekking in the Dolomites
Alta Via 2 — Trekking in the Dolomites
Day Walks in the Dolomites
Italy's Grande Traversata delle Alpi
Italy's Sibillini National Park
Ski Touring and Snowshoeing in the Dolomites
The Way of St Francis
Trekking Gran Paradiso: Alta Via 2
Trekking in the Apennines
Trekking the Giants' Trail: Alta Via 1 through the Italian Pennine Alps
Via Ferratas of the Italian Dolomites Vol 1
Vol 2
Walking in Abruzzo
Walking in Italy's Cinque Terre
Walking in Italy's Stelvio National Park
Walking in Sicily
Walking in the Aosta Valley
Walking in the Dolomites
Walking in Tuscany
Walking in Umbria
Walking Lake Como and Maggiore
Walking Lake Garda and Iseo
Walking on the Amalfi Coast
Walks and Treks in the Maritime Alps

IRELAND
The Wild Atlantic Way and Western Ireland
Walking the Kerry Way
Walking the Wicklow Way

EUROPEAN CYCLING
Cycling the Route des Grandes Alpes
Cycling the Ruta Via de la Plata
The Elbe Cycle Route
The River Loire Cycle Route
The River Rhone Cycle Route

INTERNATIONAL CHALLENGES, COLLECTIONS AND ACTIVITIES
Europe's High Points
Walking the Via Francigena Pilgrim Route —
Part 1
Part 2
Part 3

AUSTRIA
Innsbruck Mountain Adventures
Trekking Austria's Adlerweg
Trekking in Austria's Hohe Tauern
Trekking in Austria's Zillertal Alps
Trekking in the Stubai Alps
Walking in Austria
Walking in the Salzkammergut: the Austrian Lake District

MEDITERRANEAN
The High Mountains of Crete
Trekking in Greece
Walking and Trekking in Zagori
Walking and Trekking on Corfu
Walking on the Greek Islands — the Cyclades
Walking in Cyprus
Walking on Malta

HIMALAYA
8000 metres
Everest: A Trekker's Guide
Trekking in the Karakoram

NORTH AMERICA
Hiking and Cycling the California Missions Trail
The John Muir Trail
The Pacific Crest Trail

SOUTH AMERICA
Aconcagua and the Southern Andes
Hiking and Biking Peru's Inca Trails
Trekking in Torres del Paine

AFRICA
Kilimanjaro
Walking in the Drakensberg
Walks and Scrambles in the Moroccan Anti-Atlas

NEW ZEALAND AND AUSTRALIA
Hiking the Overland Track

CHINA, JAPAN, AND ASIA
Annapurna
Hiking and Trekking in the Japan Alps and Mount Fuji
Hiking in Hong Kong
Japan's Kumano Kodo Pilgrimage
Trekking in Bhutan
Trekking in Ladakh
Trekking in Tajikistan
Trekking in the Himalaya

TECHNIQUES
Fastpacking
The Mountain Hut Book

MINI GUIDES
Alpine Flowers
Navigation
Pocket First Aid and Wilderness Medicine
Snow

MOUNTAIN LITERATURE
A Walk in the Clouds
Abode of the Gods
Fifty Years of Adventure
The Pennine Way — the Path, the People, the Journey
Unjustifiable Risk?

For full information on all our guides, books and eBooks,
visit our website:
www.cicerone.co.uk

CICERONE

Trust Cicerone to guide your next adventure, wherever it may be around the world...

Discover guides for hiking, mountain walking, backpacking, trekking, trail running, cycling and mountain biking, ski touring, climbing and scrambling in Britain, Europe and worldwide.

Connect with Cicerone online and find inspiration.

- buy books and ebooks
- articles, advice and trip reports
- GPX files and updates
- regular newsletter

cicerone.co.uk